BOYHOOD

LEO TOLSTOY

TRUE SIGN
PUBLISHING HOUSE

Published by True Sign Publishing House
Address: SY. No. 21/2 & 21/3, Sonnenahalli,
Krishnarajapural, Bengaluru,
Karnataka - 560049 India
E-mail: truesignbooks@gmail.com
Website: www.truesign.in

Boyhood
Author: Leo Tolstoy

ISBN: 978-93-5462-951-8

First Edition: 2022

Contents

I. A Slow Journey 5
II. The Thunderstorm 11
III. A New Point of View 16
IV. In Moscow 20
V. My Elder Brother 22
VI. Masha 25
VII. Small Shot 27
VIII. Karl Ivanitch's History 30
IX. Continuation of Karl's Narrative 33
X. Conclusion of Karl's Narrative 36
XI. Onc Mark Only 38
XII. The Key 43
XIII. The Traitress 45
XIV. The Retribution 47
XV. Dreams 50
XVI. "Keep On Grinding, And You'll Have Flour" 54
XVII. Hatred 58
XVIII. The Maidservants' Room 60
XIX. Boyhood 65
XX. Woloda 68
XXI. Katenka And Lubotshka 71
XXII. Papa 73

XXIII. Grandmamma 76
XXIV. Myself 78
XXV. Woloda's Friends 80
XXVI. Discussions 82
XXVII. The Beginning of Our Friendship 86

I.
A Slow Journey

Again two carriages stood at the front door of the house at Petrovskoe. In one of them sat Mimi, the two girls, and their maid, with the bailiff, Jakoff, on the box, while in the other—a *britchka*—sat Woloda, myself, and our servant Vassili. Papa, who was to follow us to Moscow in a few days, was standing bareheaded on the entrance-steps. He made the sign of the cross at the windows of the carriages, and said:

"Christ go with you! Good-bye."

Jakoff and our coachman (for we had our own horses) lifted their caps in answer, and also made the sign of the cross.

"Amen. God go with us!"

The carriages began to roll away, and the birch-trees of the great avenue filed out of sight.

I was not in the least depressed on this occasion, for my mind was not so much turned upon what I had left as upon what was awaiting me. In proportion as the various objects connected with the sad recollections which had recently filled my imagination receded behind me, those recollections lost their power, and gave place to a consolatory feeling of life, youthful vigour, freshness, and hope.

Seldom have I spent four days more—well, I will not say gaily, since I should still have shrunk from appearing gay—but more agreeably and pleasantly than those occupied by our journey.

No longer were my eyes confronted with the closed door of Mamma's room (which I had never been able to pass without a pang), nor with the covered piano (which nobody opened now, and at which I could never look without trembling), nor with mourning dresses (we had each of us on our ordinary travelling clothes), nor with all those other objects which recalled to me so vividly our irreparable loss, and forced me to abstain from any manifestation of merriment lest I should unwittingly offend against *her* memory.

On the contrary, a continual succession of new and exciting objects and places now caught and held my attention, and the charms of spring awakened in my soul a soothing sense of satisfaction with the present and of blissful hope for the future.

Very early next morning the merciless Vassili (who had only just entered our service, and was therefore, like most people in such a position, zealous to a fault) came and stripped off my counterpane, affirming that it was time for me to get up, since everything was in readiness for us to continue our journey. Though I felt inclined to stretch myself and rebel—though I would gladly have spent another quarter of an hour in sweet enjoyment of my morning slumber—Vassili's inexorable face showed that he would grant me no respite, but that he was ready to tear away the counterpane twenty times more if necessary. Accordingly I submitted myself to the inevitable and ran down into the courtyard to wash myself at the fountain.

In the coffee-room, a tea-kettle was already surmounting the fire which Milka the ostler, as red in the face as a crab, was blowing with a pair of bellows. All was grey and misty in the courtyard, like steam from a smoking dunghill, but in the eastern sky the sun was diffusing a clear, cheerful radiance, and making the straw roofs of the sheds around the courtyard sparkle with the night dew. Beneath them stood our horses, tied to mangers, and I could hear the ceaseless sound of their chewing. A curly-haired dog which had been spending the night on a dry dunghill now rose in lazy fashion and, wagging its tail, walked slowly across the courtyard.

The bustling landlady opened the creaking gates, turned her meditative cows into the street (whence came the lowing and bellowing of other cattle), and exchanged a word or two with a sleepy neighbour. Philip, with his shirt-sleeves rolled up, was working the windlass of a draw-well, and sending sparkling fresh water coursing into an oaken trough, while in the pool beneath it some early-rising ducks were taking a bath. It gave me pleasure to watch his strongly-marked, bearded face, and the veins and muscles as they stood out upon his great powerful hands whenever he made an extra effort. In the room behind the partition-wall where Mimi and the girls had slept (yet so near to ourselves that we had exchanged confidences overnight) movements now became audible, their maid kept passing in and out with clothes, and, at last the door opened and we were summoned to breakfast. Woloda, however, remained in a state of bustle throughout as he ran to fetch first one article and then another and urged the maid to hasten her preparations.

The horses were put to, and showed their impatience by tinkling their bells. Parcels, trunks, dressing-cases, and boxes were replaced, and we set about taking our seats. Yet, every time that we got in, the mountain of luggage in the *britchka* seemed to have grown larger than before, and we had much ado to understand how things had been arranged yesterday, and how we should sit now. A tea-chest, in particular, greatly inconvenienced me, but Vassili declared that "things will soon right themselves," and I had no choice but to believe him.

The sun was just rising, covered with dense white clouds, and every object around us was standing out in a cheerful, calm sort of radiance. The whole was beautiful to look at, and I felt comfortable and light of heart.

Before us the road ran like a broad, sinuous ribbon through cornfields glittering with dew. Here and there a dark bush or young birch-tree cast a long shadow over the ruts and scattered grass-tufts of the track. Yet even the monotonous din of our carriage-wheels and collar-bells could not drown the joyous song of soaring larks, nor the combined odour of moth-eaten cloth, dust, and sourness peculiar to our *britchka* overpower the fresh scents of the morning. I felt in my heart that delightful impulse to be up and doing which is a sign of sincere enjoyment.

As I had not been able to say my prayers in the courtyard of the inn, but had nevertheless been assured once that on the very first day when I omitted to perform that ceremony some misfortune would overtake me, I now hastened to rectify the omission. Taking off my cap, and stooping down in a corner of the *britchka*, I duly recited my orisons, and unobtrusively signed the sign of the cross beneath my coat. Yet all the while a thousand different objects were distracting my attention, and more than once I inadvertently repeated a prayer twice over.

Soon on the little footpath beside the road became visible some slowly moving figures. They were pilgrims. On their heads they had dirty handkerchiefs, on their backs wallets of birch-bark, and on their feet bundles of soiled rags and heavy bast shoes. Moving their staffs in regular rhythm, and scarcely throwing us a glance, they pressed onwards with heavy tread and in single file.

"Where have they come from?" I wondered to myself, "and whither are they bound? Is it a long pilgrimage they are making?" But soon the shadows they cast on the road became indistinguishable from the shadows of the bushes which they passed.

Next a carriage-and-four could be seen approaching us. In two seconds the faces which looked out at us from it with smiling curiosity had vanished. How strange it seemed that those faces should have nothing in common with me, and that in all probability they would never meet my eyes again!

Next came a pair of post-horses, with the traces looped up to their collars. On one of them a young postillion—his lamb's wool cap cocked to one side—was negligently kicking his booted legs against the flanks of his steed as he sang a melancholy ditty. Yet his face and attitude seemed to me to express such perfect carelessness and indolent ease that I imagined it to be the height of happiness to be a postillion and to sing melancholy songs.

Far off, through a cutting in the road, there soon stood out against the light-blue sky, the green roof of a village church. Presently the village itself became visible, together with the roof of the manor-house and the garden attached to it. Who lived in that house? Children, parents, teachers? Why should we not call there and make the acquaintance of its inmates?

Next we overtook a file of loaded waggons—a procession to which our vehicles had to yield the road.

"What have you got in there?" asked Vassili of one waggoner who was dangling his legs lazily over the splashboard of his conveyance and flicking his whip about as he gazed at us with a stolid, vacant look; but he only made answer when we were too far off to catch what he said.

"And what have *you* got?" asked Vassili of a second waggoner who was lying at full length under a new rug on the driving-seat of his vehicle. The red poll and red face beneath it lifted themselves up for a second from the folds of the rug, measured our *britchka* with a cold, contemptuous look, and lay down again; whereupon I concluded that the driver was wondering to himself who we were, whence we had come, and whither we were going.

These various objects of interest had absorbed so much of my time that, as yet, I had paid no attention to the crooked figures on the verst posts as we passed them in rapid succession; but in time the sun began to burn my head and back, the road to become increasingly dusty, the impedimenta in the carriage to grow more and more uncomfortable, and myself to feel more and more cramped. Consequently, I relapsed into devoting my whole faculties to the distance-posts and their numerals, and to solving difficult mathematical problems for reckoning the time when we should arrive at the next posting-house.

"Twelve versts are a third of thirty-six, and in all there are forty-one to Lipetz. We have done a third and how much, then?", and so forth, and so forth.

"Vassili," was my next remark, on observing that he was beginning to nod on the box-seat, "suppose we change seats? Will you?" Vassili agreed, and had no sooner stretched himself out in the body of the vehicle than he began to snore. To me on my new perch, however, a most interesting spectacle now became visible—namely, our horses, all of which were familiar to me down to the smallest detail.

"Why is Diashak on the right today, Philip, not on the left?" I asked knowingly. "And Nerusinka is not doing her proper share of the pulling."

"One could not put Diashak on the left," replied Philip, altogether ignoring my last remark. "He is not the kind of horse to put there at all. A horse like the one on the left now is the right kind of one for the job."

After this fragment of eloquence, Philip turned towards Diashak and began to do his best to worry the poor animal by jogging at the reins, in spite of the fact that Diashak was doing well and dragging the vehicle almost unaided. This Philip continued to do until he found it convenient to breathe and rest himself awhile and to settle his cap askew, though it had looked well enough before.

I profited by the opportunity to ask him to let me have the reins to hold, until, the whole six in my hand, as well as the whip, I had attained complete happiness. Several times I asked whether I was doing things right, but, as usual, Philip was never satisfied, and soon destroyed my felicity.

The heat increased until a hand showed itself at the carriage window, and waved a bottle and a parcel of eatables; whereupon Vassili leapt briskly from the *britchka*, and ran forward to get us something to eat and drink.

When we arrived at a steep descent, we all got out and ran down it to a little bridge, while Vassili and Jakoff followed, supporting the carriage on either side, as though to hold it up in the event of its threatening to upset.

After that, Mimi gave permission for a change of seats, and sometimes Woloda or myself would ride in the carriage, and Lubotshka or Katenka in the *britchka*. This arrangement greatly pleased the girls, since much more fun went on in the *britchka*. Just when the day was at its hottest, we got out at a wood, and, breaking off a quantity of branches, transformed our vehicle into a bower. This travelling arbour then bustled on to catch the carriage up, and had the effect of exciting Lubotshka to one of those piercing shrieks of delight which she was in the habit of occasionally emitting.

At last we drew near the village where we were to halt and dine. Already we could perceive the smell of the place—the smell of smoke and tar and sheep—and distinguish the sound of voices, footsteps, and carts. The bells on our horses began to ring less clearly than they had done in the open country, and on both sides the road became lined with huts—dwellings with straw roofs, carved porches, and small red or green painted shutters to the windows, through which, here and there, was a woman's face looking inquisitively out. Peasant children clad in smocks only stood staring open-eyed or, stretching out their arms to us, ran barefooted through the dust to climb on to the luggage behind, despite Philip's menacing gestures. Likewise, red-haired waiters came darting around the carriages to invite us, with words and signs, to select their several hostelries as our halting-place.

Presently a gate creaked, and we entered a courtyard. Four hours of rest and liberty now awaited us.

II.
The Thunderstorm

The sun was sinking towards the west, and his long, hot rays were burning my neck and cheeks beyond endurance, while thick clouds of dust were rising from the road and filling the whole air. Not the slightest wind was there to carry it away. I could not think what to do. Neither the dust-blackened face of Woloda dozing in a corner, nor the motion of Philip's back, nor the long shadow of our *britchka* as it came bowling along behind us brought me any relief. I concentrated my whole attention upon the distance-posts ahead and the clouds which, hitherto dispersed over the sky, were now assuming a menacing blackness, and beginning to form themselves into a single solid mass.

From time to time distant thunder could be heard—a circumstance which greatly increased my impatience to arrive at the inn where we were to spend the night. A thunderstorm always communicated to me an inexpressibly oppressive feeling of fear and gloom.

Yet we were still ten versts from the next village, and in the meanwhile the large purple cloudbank—arisen from no one knows where—was advancing steadily towards us. The sun, not yet obscured, was picking out its fuscous shape with dazzling light, and marking its front with grey stripes running right down to the horizon. At intervals, vivid lightning could be seen in the distance, followed by low rumbles which increased steadily in volume until they merged into a prolonged roll which seemed to embrace the entire heavens. At length, Vassili got up and covered over the *britchka*, the coachman wrapped himself up in his cloak and lifted his cap to make the sign of the cross at each successive thunderclap, and the horses pricked up their ears and snorted as though to drink in the fresh air which the flying clouds were outdistancing. The *britchka* began to roll more swiftly along the dusty road, and I felt uneasy, and as though the blood were coursing more quickly through my veins. Soon the clouds had veiled the face of the sun, and though he threw a last gleam of light to the dark and terrifying horizon, he had no choice but to disappear behind them.

Suddenly everything around us seemed changed, and assumed a gloomy aspect. A wood of aspen trees which we were passing seemed to be all in a tremble, with its leaves showing white against the dark lilac background of the clouds, murmuring together in an agitated manner. The tops of the larger trees began to bend to and fro, and dried leaves and grass to whirl about in eddies over the road. Swallows and white-breasted swifts came darting around the *britchka* and even passing in front of the forelegs of the horses. While rooks, despite their outstretched wings, were laid, as it were, on their keels by the wind. Finally, the leather apron which covered us began to flutter about and to beat against the sides of the conveyance.

The lightning flashed right into the *britchka* as, cleaving the obscurity for a second, it lit up the grey cloth and silk galloon of the lining and Woloda's figure pressed back into a corner.

Next came a terrible sound which, rising higher and higher, and spreading further and further, increased until it reached its climax in a deafening thunderclap which made us tremble and hold our breaths. "The wrath of God"—what poetry there is in that simple popular conception!

The pace of the vehicle was continually increasing, and from Philip's and Vassili's backs (the former was tugging furiously at the reins) I could see that they too were alarmed.

Bowling rapidly down an incline, the *britchka* cannoned violently against a wooden bridge at the bottom. I dared not stir and expected destruction every moment.

Crack! A trace had given way, and, in spite of the ceaseless, deafening thunderclaps, we had to pull up on the bridge.

Leaning my head despairingly against the side of the *britchka*, I followed with a beating heart the movements of Philip's great black fingers as he tied up the broken trace and, with hands and the butt-end of the whip, pushed the harness vigorously back into its place.

My sense of terror was increasing with the violence of the thunder. Indeed, at the moment of supreme silence which generally precedes the greatest intensity of a storm, it mounted to such a height that I felt as though another quarter of an hour of this emotion would kill me.

Just then there appeared from beneath the bridge a human being who, clad in a torn, filthy smock, and supported on a pair of thin shanks bare of muscles, thrust an idiotic face, a tremulous, bare, shaven head, and a pair of red, shining stumps in place of hands into the *britchka*.

"M-my lord! A copeck for—for God's sake!" groaned a feeble voice as at each word the wretched being made the sign of the cross and bowed himself to the ground.

I cannot describe the chill feeling of horror which penetrated my heart at that moment. A shudder crept through all my hair, and my eyes stared in vacant terror at the outcast.

Vassili, who was charged with the apportioning of alms during the journey, was busy helping Philip, and only when everything had been put straight and Philip had resumed the reins again had he time to look for his purse. Hardly had the *britchka* begun to move when a blinding flash filled the welkin with a blaze of light which brought the horses to their haunches. Then, the flash was followed by such an ear-splitting roar that the very vault of heaven seemed to be descending upon our heads. The wind blew harder than ever, and Vassili's cloak, the manes and tails of the horses, and the carriage-apron were all slanted in one direction as they waved furiously in the violent blast.

Presently, upon the *britchka's* top there fell some large drops of rain—"one, two, three:" then suddenly, and as though a roll of drums were being beaten over our heads, the whole countryside resounded with the clatter of the deluge.

From Vassili's movements, I could see that he had now got his purse open, and that the poor outcast was still bowing and making the sign of the cross as he ran beside the wheels of the vehicle, at the imminent risk of being run over, and reiterated from time to time his plea, "For-for God's sake!" At last a copeck rolled upon the ground, and the miserable creature—his mutilated arms, with their sleeves wet through and through, held out before him—stopped perplexed in the roadway and vanished from my sight.

The heavy rain, driven before the tempestuous wind, poured down in pailfuls and, dripping from Vassili's thick cloak, formed a series of pools on the apron. The dust became changed to a paste which clung to the wheels, and the ruts became transformed into muddy rivulets.

At last, however, the lightning grew paler and more diffuse, and the thunderclaps lost some of their terror amid the monotonous rattling of the downpour. Then the rain also abated, and the clouds began to disperse. In the region of the sun, a lightness appeared, and between the white-grey clouds could be caught glimpses of an azure sky.

Finally, a dazzling ray shot across the pools on the road, shot through the threads of rain—now falling thin and straight, as from a sieve—, and fell upon the fresh leaves and blades of grass. The great cloud was still louring black and threatening on the far horizon, but I no longer felt afraid of it—I felt only an inexpressibly pleasant hopefulness in proportion, as trust in life replaced the late burden of fear. Indeed, my heart was smiling like that of refreshed, revivified Nature herself.

Vassili took off his cloak and wrung the water from it. Woloda flung back the apron, and I stood up in the *britchka* to drink in the new, fresh, balm-laden air. In front of us was the carriage, rolling along and looking as wet and resplendent in the sunlight as though it had just been polished. On one side of the road boundless oatfields, intersected in places by small ravines which now showed bright with their moist earth and greenery, stretched to the far horizon like a checkered carpet, while on the other side of us an aspen wood, intermingled with hazel bushes, and parquetted with wild thyme in joyous profusion, no longer rustled and trembled, but slowly dropped rich, sparkling diamonds from its newly-bathed branches on to the withered leaves of last year.

From above us, from every side, came the happy songs of little birds calling to one another among the dripping brushwood, while clear from the inmost depths of the wood sounded the voice of the cuckoo. So delicious was the wondrous scent of the wood, the scent which follows a thunderstorm in spring, the scent of birch-trees, violets, mushrooms, and thyme, that I could no longer remain in the *britchka*. Jumping out, I ran to some bushes, and, regardless of the showers of drops discharged upon me, tore off a few sprigs of thyme, and buried my face in them to smell their glorious scent.

Then, despite the mud which had got into my boots, as also the fact that my stockings were soaked, I went skipping through the puddles to the window of the carriage.

“Lubotshka! Katenka!” I shouted as I handed them some of the thyme, “Just look how delicious this is!”

The girls smelt it and cried, “A-ah!” but Mimi shrieked to me to go away, for fear I should be run over by the wheels.

“Oh, but smell how delicious it is!” I persisted.

III.
A New Point of View

Katenka was with me in the *britchka;* her lovely head inclined as she gazed pensively at the roadway. I looked at her in silence and wondered what had brought the unchildlike expression of sadness to her face which I now observed for the first time there.

"We shall soon be in Moscow," I said at last. "How large do you suppose it is?"

"I don't know," she replied.

"Well, but how large do you *imagine?* As large as Serpukhov?"

"What do you say?"

"Nothing."

Yet the instinctive feeling which enables one person to guess the thoughts of another and serves as a guiding thread in conversation soon made Katenka feel that her indifference was disagreeable to me; wherefore she raised her head presently, and, turning round, said:

"Did your Papa tell you that we girls too were going to live at your Grandmamma's?"

"Yes, he said that we should *all* live there."

"*All* live there?"

"Yes, of course. We shall have one half of the upper floor, and you the other half, and Papa the wing; but we shall all of us dine together with Grandmamma downstairs."

"But Mamma says that your Grandmamma is so very grave and so easily made angry?"

"No, she only *seems* like that at first. She is grave, but not bad-tempered. On the contrary, she is both kind and cheerful. If you could only have seen the ball at her house!"

"All the same, I am afraid of her. Besides, who knows whether we—"

Katenka stopped short, and once again became thoughtful.

"What?" I asked with some anxiety.

"Nothing, I only said that—"

"No. You said, 'Who knows whether we—'"

"And *you* said, didn't you, that once there was ever such a ball at Grandmamma's?"

"Yes. It is a pity you were not there. There were heaps of guests—about a thousand people, and all of them princes or generals, and there was music, and I danced—But, Katenka" I broke off, "you are not listening to me?"

"Oh yes, I am listening. You said that you danced—?"

"Why are you so serious?"

"Well, one cannot *always* be gay."

"But you have changed tremendously since Woloda and I first went to Moscow. Tell me the truth, now: why are you so odd?" My tone was resolute.

"*Am* I so odd?" said Katenka with an animation which showed me that my question had interested her. "I don't see that I am so at all."

"Well, you are not the same as you were before," I continued. "Once upon a time any one could see that you were our equal in everything, and that you loved us like relations, just as we did you; but now you are always serious, and keep yourself apart from us."

"Oh, not at all."

"But let me finish, please," I interrupted, already conscious of a slight tickling in my nose—the precursor of the tears which usually came to my eyes whenever I had to vent any long pent-up feeling. "You avoid us, and talk to no one but Mimi, as though you had no wish for our further acquaintance."

"But one cannot always remain the same—one *must* change a little sometimes," replied Katenka, who had an inveterate habit of pleading some such fatalistic necessity whenever she did not know what else to say.

I recollect that once, when having a quarrel with Lubotshka, who had called her "a stupid girl," she (Katenka) retorted that *everybody* could not be wise, seeing that a certain number of stupid people was a necessity in the world. However, on the present occasion, I was not satisfied that any such inevitable necessity for "changing sometimes" existed, and asked further:

"*Why* is it necessary?"

"Well, you see, we *may* not always go on living together as we are doing now," said Katenka, colouring slightly, and regarding Philip's back with a grave expression on her face. "My Mamma was able to live with your mother because she was her friend; but will a similar arrangement always suit the Countess, who, they say, is so easily offended? Besides, in any case, we shall have to separate *some* day. You are rich—you have Petrovskoe, while we are poor—Mamma has nothing."

"You are rich," "we are poor"—both the words and the ideas which they connoted seemed to me extremely strange. Hitherto, I had conceived that only beggars and peasants were poor and could not reconcile in my mind the idea of poverty and the graceful, charming Katenka. I felt that Mimi and her daughter ought to live with us *always* and to share everything that we possessed. Things ought never to be otherwise. Yet, at this moment, a thousand new thoughts with regard to their lonely position came crowding into my head, and I felt so remorseful at the notion that we were rich and they poor, that I coloured up and could not look Katenka in the face.

"Yet what does it matter," I thought, "that we are well off and they are not? Why should that necessitate a separation? Why should we not share in common what we possess?" Yet, I had a feeling that I could not talk to Katenka on the subject, since a certain practical instinct, opposed to all logical reasoning, warned me that, right though she possibly was, I should do wrong to tell her so.

"It is impossible that you should leave us. How could we ever live apart?"

"Yet what else is there to be done? Certainly I do not *want* to do it; yet, if it *has* to be done, I know what my plan in life will be."

"Yes, to become an actress! How absurd!" I exclaimed (for I knew that to enter that profession had always been her favourite dream).

"Oh no. I only used to say that when I was a little girl."

"Well, then? What?"

"To go into a convent and live there. Then I could walk out in a black dress and velvet cap!" cried Katenka.

Has it ever befallen you, my readers, to become suddenly aware that your conception of things has altered—as though every object in life had unexpectedly turned a side towards you of which you had hitherto remained unaware? Such a species of moral change occurred, as regards myself, during this journey, and therefore from it I date the beginning of my boyhood. For the first time in my life, I then envisaged the idea that we—*i.e.* our family—were not the only persons in the world; that not every conceivable interest was centred in ourselves; and that there existed numbers of people who had nothing in common with us, cared nothing for us, and even knew nothing of our existence. No doubt I had known all this before—only I had not known it then as I knew it now; I had never properly felt or understood it.

Thought merges into conviction through paths of its own, as well as, sometimes, with great suddenness and by methods wholly different from those which have brought other intellects to the same conclusion. For me the conversation with Katenka—striking deeply as it did, and forcing me to reflect on her future position—constituted such a path. As I gazed at the towns and villages through which we passed, and in each house of which lived at least one family like our own, as well as at the women and children who stared with curiosity at our carriages and then became lost to sight for ever, and the peasants and workmen who did not even look at us, much less make us any obeisance, the question arose for the first time in my thoughts, "Whom else do they care for if not for us?" And this question was followed by others, such as, "To what end do they live?" "How do they educate their children?" "Do they teach their children and let them play? What are their names?" and so forth.

IV.
In Moscow

From the time of our arrival in Moscow, the change in my conception of objects, of persons, and of my connection with them became increasingly perceptible. When at my first meeting with Grandmamma, I saw her thin, wrinkled face and faded eyes, the mingled respect and fear with which she had hitherto inspired me gave place to compassion, and when, laying her cheek against Lubotshka's head, she sobbed as though she saw before her the corpse of her beloved daughter, my compassion grew to love.

I felt deeply sorry to see her grief at our meeting, even though I knew that in ourselves we represented nothing in her eyes, but were dear to her only as reminders of our mother—that every kiss which she imprinted upon my cheeks expressed the one thought, "She is no more—she is dead, and I shall never see her again."

Papa, who took little notice of us here in Moscow, and whose face was perpetually preoccupied on the rare occasions when he came in his black dress-coat to take formal dinner with us, lost much in my eyes at this period, in spite of his turned-up ruffles, *robes de chambre*, overseers, bailiffs, expeditions to the estate, and hunting exploits.

Karl Ivanitch—whom Grandmamma always called "Uncle," and who (Heaven knows why!) had taken it into his head to adorn the bald pate of my childhood's days with a red wig parted in the middle—now looked to me so strange and ridiculous that I wondered how I could ever have failed to observe the fact before. Even between the girls and ourselves there seemed to have sprung up an invisible barrier. They, too, began to have secrets among themselves, as well as to evince a desire to show off their ever-lengthening skirts even as we boys did our trousers and ankle-straps. As for Mimi, she appeared at luncheon, the first Sunday, in such a gorgeous dress and with so many ribbons in her cap that it was clear that we were no longer *en campagne*, and that everything was now going to be different.

V.

My Elder Brother

I was only a year and some odd months younger than Woloda, and from the first we had grown up and studied and played together. Hitherto, the difference between elder and younger brother had never been felt between us, but at the period of which I am speaking, I began to have a notion that I was not Woloda's equal either in years, in tastes, or in capabilities. I even began to fancy that Woloda himself was aware of his superiority and that he was proud of it, and, though, perhaps, I was wrong, the idea wounded my conceit—already suffering from frequent comparison with him. He was my superior in everything—in games, in studies, in quarrels, and in deportment. All this brought about an estrangement between us and occasioned me moral sufferings which I had never hitherto experienced.

When for the first time Woloda wore Dutch pleated shirts, I at once said that I was greatly put out at not being given similar ones, and each time that he arranged his collar, I felt that he was doing so on purpose to offend me. But, what tormented me most of all was the idea that Woloda could see through me, yet did not choose to show it.

Who has not known those secret, wordless communications which spring from some barely perceptible smile or movement—from a casual glance between two persons who live as constantly together as do brothers, friends, man and wife, or master and servant—particularly if those two persons do not in all things cultivate mutual frankness? How many half-expressed wishes, thoughts, and meanings which one shrinks from revealing are made plain by a single accidental glance which timidly and irresolutely meets the eye!

However, in my own case I may have been deceived by my excessive capacity for, and love of, analysis. Possibly Woloda did not feel at all as I did. Passionate and frank, but unstable in his likings, he was attracted by the most diverse things, and always surrendered himself wholly to such attraction. For instance, he suddenly conceived a passion for pictures, spent all his money on their purchase, begged Papa, Grandmamma, and his drawing master to add to their number, and applied himself with enthusiasm to art. Next came a sudden rage for curios, with which he covered his table, and for which he ransacked the whole house. Following upon that, he took to violent novel-reading—procuring such works by stealth, and devouring them day and night. Involuntarily I was influenced by his whims, for, though too proud to imitate him, I was also too young and too lacking in independence to choose my own way. Above all, I envied Woloda his happy, nobly frank character, which showed itself most strikingly when we quarrelled. I always felt that he was in the right, yet could not imitate him. For instance, on one occasion when his passion for curios was at its height, I went to his table and accidentally broke an empty many-coloured smelling-bottle.

"Who gave you leave to touch my things?" asked Woloda, chancing to enter the room at that moment and at once perceiving the disorder which I had occasioned in the orderly arrangement of the treasures on his table. "And where is that smelling bottle? Perhaps you—?"

"I let it fall, and it smashed to pieces; but what does that matter?"

"Well, please do me the favour never to *dare* to touch my things again," he said as he gathered up the broken fragments and looked at them vexedly.

"And will *you* please do me the favour never to *order* me to do anything whatever," I retorted. "When a thing's broken, it's broken, and there is no more to be said." Then I smiled, though I hardly felt like smiling.

"Oh, it may mean nothing to you, but to me it means a good deal," said Woloda, shrugging his shoulders (a habit he had caught from Papa). "First of all you go and break my things, and then you laugh. What a nuisance a little boy can be!"

"*Little* boy, indeed? Then *you*, I suppose, are a man, and ever so wise?"

"I do not intend to quarrel with you," said Woloda, giving me a slight push. "Go away."

"Don't you push me!"

"Go away."

"I say again—don't you push me!"

Woloda took me by the hand and tried to drag me away from the table, but I was excited to the last degree, and gave the table such a push with my foot that I upset the whole concern, and brought china and crystal ornaments and everything else with a crash to the floor.

"You disgusting little brute!" exclaimed Woloda, trying to save some of his falling treasures.

"At last all is over between us," I thought to myself as I strode from the room. "We are separated now for ever."

It was not until evening that we again exchanged a word. Yet I felt guilty, and was afraid to look at him, and remained at a loose end all day.

Woloda, on the contrary, did his lessons as diligently as ever, and passed the time after luncheon in talking and laughing with the girls. As soon, again, as afternoon lessons were over I left the room, for it would have been terribly embarrassing for me to be alone with my brother. When, too, the evening class in history was ended I took my notebook and moved towards the door. Just as I passed Woloda, I pouted and pulled an angry face, though in reality I should have liked to have made my peace with him. At the same moment he lifted his head, and with a barely perceptible and good-humouredly satirical smile looked me full in the face. Our eyes met, and I saw that he understood me, while he, for his part, saw that I knew that he understood me; yet a feeling stronger than myself obliged me to turn away from him.

"Nicolinka," he said in a perfectly simple and anything but mock-pathetic way, "you have been angry with me long enough. I am sorry if I offended you," and he tendered me his hand.

It was as though something welled up from my heart and nearly choked me. Presently it passed away, the tears rushed to my eyes, and I felt immensely relieved.

"I too am so-rry, Wo-lo-da," I said, taking his hand. Yet he only looked at me with an expression as though he could not understand why there should be tears in my eyes.

VI.
Masha

None of the changes produced in my conception of things were so striking as the one which led me to cease to see in one of our chambermaids a mere servant of the female sex, but, on the contrary, a *woman* upon whom depended, to a certain extent, my peace of mind and happiness. From the time of my earliest recollection I can remember Masha an inmate of our house, yet never until the occurrence of which I am going to speak—an occurrence which entirely altered my impression of her—had I bestowed the smallest attention upon her. She was twenty-five years old, while I was but fourteen. Also, she was very beautiful. But I hesitate to give a further description of her lest my imagination should once more picture the bewitching, though deceptive, conception of her which filled my mind during the period of my passion. To be frank, I will only say that she was extraordinarily handsome, magnificently developed, and a *woman*—as also that I was but fourteen.

At one of those moments when, lesson-book in hand, I would pace the room, and try to keep strictly to one particular crack in the floor as I hummed a fragment of some tune or repeated some vague formula—in short, at one of those moments when the mind leaves off thinking and the imagination gains the upper hand and yearns for new impressions—I left the schoolroom, and turned, with no definite purpose in view, towards the head of the staircase.

Somebody in slippers was ascending the second flight of stairs. Of course I felt curious to see who it was, but the footsteps ceased abruptly, and then I heard Masha's voice say:

"Go away! What nonsense! What would Maria Ivanovna think if she were to come now?"

"Oh, but she will not come," answered Woloda's voice in a whisper.

"Well, go away, you silly boy," and Masha came running up, and fled past me.

I cannot describe the way in which this discovery confounded me. Nevertheless the feeling of amazement soon gave place to a kind of sympathy with Woloda's conduct. I found myself wondering less at the conduct itself than at his ability to behave so agreeably. Also, I found myself involuntarily desiring to imitate him.

Sometimes I would pace the landing for an hour at a time, with no other thought in my head than to watch for movements from above. Yet, although I longed beyond all things to do as Woloda had done, I could not bring myself to the point. At other times, filled with a sense of envious jealousy, I would conceal myself behind a door and listen to the sounds which came from the maidservants' room, until the thought would occur to my mind, "How if I were to go in now and, like Woloda, kiss Masha? What should I say when she asked me—*me* with the huge nose and the tuft on the top of my head—what I wanted?" Sometimes, too, I could hear her saying to Woloda,

"That serves you right! Go away! Nicolas Petrovitch never comes in here with such nonsense." Alas! she did not know that Nicolas Petrovitch was sitting on the staircase just below and feeling that he would give all he possessed to be in "that bold fellow Woloda's" place! I was shy by nature, and rendered worse in that respect by a consciousness of my own ugliness. I am certain that nothing so much influences the development of a man as his exterior—though the exterior itself less than his belief in its plainness or beauty.

Yet I was too conceited altogether to resign myself to my fate. I tried to comfort myself much as the fox did when he declared that the grapes were sour. That is to say, I tried to make light of the satisfaction to be gained from making such use of a pleasing exterior as I believed Woloda to employ (satisfaction which I nevertheless envied him from my heart), and endeavoured with every faculty of my intellect and imagination to console myself with a pride in my isolation.

VII.
Small Shot

"Good gracious! Powder!" exclaimed Mimi in a voice trembling with alarm. "Whatever are you doing? You will set the house on fire in a moment, and be the death of us all!" Upon that, with an indescribable expression of firmness, Mimi ordered every one to stand aside, and, regardless of all possible danger from a premature explosion, strode with long and resolute steps to where some small shot was scattered about the floor, and began to trample upon it.

When, in her opinion, the peril was at least lessened, she called for Michael and commanded him to throw the "powder" away into some remote spot, or, better still, to immerse it in water; after which she adjusted her cap and returned proudly to the drawing-room, murmuring as she went, "At least I can say that they are well looked after."

When Papa issued from his room and took us to see Grandmamma we found Mimi sitting by the window and glancing with a grave, mysterious, official expression towards the door. In her hand she was holding something carefully wrapped in paper. I guessed that that something was the small shot, and that Grandmamma had been informed of the occurrence. In the room also were the maidservant Gasha (who, to judge by her angry flushed face, was in a state of great irritation) and Doctor Blumenthal—the latter a little man pitted with smallpox, who was endeavouring by tacit, pacificatory signs with his head and eyes to reassure the perturbed Gasha. Grandmamma was sitting a little askew and playing that variety of "patience" which is called "The Traveller"—two unmistakable signs of her displeasure.

"How are you to-day, Mamma?" said Papa as he kissed her hand respectfully. "Have you had a good night?"

"Yes, very good, my dear; you *know* that I always enjoy sound health," replied Grandmamma in a tone implying that Papa's inquiries were out of place and highly offensive. "Please give me a clean pocket-handkerchief," she added to Gasha.

"I *have* given you one, madam," answered Gasha, pointing to the snow-white cambric handkerchief which she had just laid on the arm of Grandmamma's chair.

"No, no; it's a nasty, dirty thing. Take it away and bring me a *clean* one, my dear."

Gasha went to a cupboard and slammed the door of it back so violently that every window rattled. Grandmamma glared angrily at each of us, and then turned her attention to following the movements of the servant. After the latter had presented her with what I suspected to be the same handkerchief as before, Grandmamma continued:

"And when do you mean to cut me some snuff, my dear?"

"When I have time."

"What do you say?"

"To-day."

"If you don't want to continue in my service you had better say so at once. I would have sent you away long ago had I known that you wished it."

"It wouldn't have broken my heart if you had!" muttered the woman in an undertone.

Here the doctor winked at her again, but she returned his gaze so firmly and wrathfully that he soon lowered it and went on playing with his watch-key.

"You see, my dear, how people speak to me in my own house!" said Grandmamma to Papa when Gasha had left the room grumbling.

"Well, Mamma, I will cut you some snuff myself," replied Papa, though evidently at a loss how to proceed now that he had made this rash promise.

"No, no, I thank you. Probably she is cross because she knows that no one except herself can cut the snuff just as I like it. Do you know, my dear," she went on after a pause, "that your children very nearly set the house on fire this morning?"

Papa gazed at Grandmamma with respectful astonishment.

"Yes, they were playing with something or another. Tell him the story," she added to Mimi.

Papa could not help smiling as he took the shot in his hand.

"This is only small shot, Mamma," he remarked, "and could never be dangerous."

"I thank you, my dear, for your instruction, but I am rather too old for that sort of thing."

"Nerves, nerves!" whispered the doctor.

Papa turned to us and asked us where we had got the stuff, and how we could dare to play with it.

"Don't ask *them*, ask that useless 'Uncle,' rather," put in Grandmamma, laying a peculiar stress upon the word "*Uncle*." "What else is he for?"

"Woloda says that Karl Ivanitch gave him the powder himself," declared Mimi.

"Then you can see for yourself what use he is," continued Grandmamma. "And where IS he—this precious 'Uncle'? How is one to get hold of him? Send him here."

"He has gone an errand for me," said Papa.

"That is not at all right," rejoined Grandmamma. "He ought *always* to be here. True, the children are yours, not mine, and I have nothing to do with them, seeing that you are so much cleverer than I am; yet all the same I think it is time we had a regular tutor for them, and not this 'Uncle' of a German—a stupid fellow who knows only how to teach them rude manners and Tyrolean songs! Is it necessary, I ask you, that they should learn Tyrolean songs? However, there is no one for me to consult about it, and you must do just as you like."

The word "*now*" meant "*now that they have no mother*," and suddenly awakened sad recollections in Grandmamma's heart. She threw a glance at the snuff-box bearing Mamma's portrait and sighed.

"I thought of all this long ago," said Papa eagerly, "as well as taking your advice on the subject. How would you like St. Jerome to superintend their lessons?"

"Oh, I think he would do excellently, my friend," said Grandmamma in a mollified tone, "He is at least a tutor *comme il faut*, and knows how to instruct *des enfants de bonne maison*. He is not a mere 'Uncle' who is good only for taking them out walking."

"Very well; I will talk to him to-morrow," said Papa. And, sure enough, two days later saw Karl Ivanitch forced to retire in favour of the young Frenchman referred to.

VIII.
Karl Ivanitch's History

Thhw evening before the day when Karl was to leave us for ever, he was standing (clad, as usual, in his wadded dressing-gown and red cap) near the bed in his room, and bending down over a trunk as he carefully packed his belongings.

His behaviour towards us had been very cool of late, and he had seemed to shrink from all contact with us. Consequently, when I entered his room on the present occasion, he only glanced at me for a second and then went on with his occupation. Even though I proceeded to jump on to his bed (a thing hitherto always forbidden me to do), he said not a word; and the idea that he would soon be scolding or forgiving us no longer—no longer having anything to do with us—reminded me vividly of the impending separation. I felt grieved to think that he had ceased to love us and wanted to show him my grief.

"Will you let me help you?" I said, approaching him.

He looked at me for a moment and turned away again. Yet the expression of pain in his eyes showed that his coldness was not the result of indifference, but rather of sincere and concentrated sorrow.

"God sees and knows everything," he said at length, raising himself to his full height and drawing a deep sigh. "Yes, Nicolinka," he went on, observing, the expression of sincere pity on my face, "my fate has been an unhappy one from the cradle, and will continue so to the grave. The good that I have done to people has always been repaid with evil; yet, though I shall receive no reward here, I shall find one *there*" (he pointed upwards). "Ah, if only you knew my whole story, and all that I have endured in this life!—I who have been a bootmaker, a soldier, a deserter, a factory hand, and a teacher! Yet now—now I am nothing, and, like the Son of Man, have nowhere to lay my head." Sitting down upon a chair, he covered his eyes with his hand.

Seeing that he was in the introspective mood in which a man pays no attention to his listener as he cons over his secret thoughts, I remained silent, and, seating myself upon the bed, continued to watch his kind face.

"You are no longer a child. You can understand things now, and I will tell you my whole story and all that I have undergone. Some day, my children, you may remember the old friend who loved you so much—"

He leant his elbow upon the table by his side, took a pinch of snuff, and, in the peculiarly measured, guttural tone in which he used to dictate us our lessons, began the story of his career.

Since he many times in later years repeated the whole to me again—always in the same order, and with the same expressions and the same unvarying intonation—I will try to render it literally, and without omitting the innumerable grammatical errors into which he always strayed when speaking in Russian. Whether it was really the history of his life, or whether it was the mere product of his imagination—that is to say, some narrative which he had conceived during his lonely residence in our house, and had at last, from endless repetition, come to believe in himself—or whether he was adorning with imaginary facts the true record of his career, I have never quite been able to make out. On the one hand, there was too much depth of feeling and practical consistency in its recital for it to be wholly incredible, while, on the other hand, the abundance of poetical beauty which it contained tended to raise doubts in the mind of the listener.

"Me vere very unhappy from ze time of my birth," he began with a profound sigh. "Ze noble blot of ze Countess of Zomerblat flows in my veins. Me vere born six veek after ze vetting. Ze man of my *Mutter* (I called him 'Papa') vere farmer to ze Count von Zomerblat. He coult not forget my *Mutter's* shame, ant loaft me not. I had a youngster broser Johann ant two sister, pot me vere strange petween my own family. Ven Johann mate several silly trick Papa sayt, 'Wit sis chilt Karl I am never to have one moment tranquil!' and zen he scoltet and ponishet me. Ven ze sister quarrellet among zemselves Papa sayt, 'Karl vill never be one opedient poy,' ant still scoltet ant ponishet me. My goot Mamma alone loaft ant tenteret me. Often she sayt to me, 'Karl, come in my room,' ant zere she kisset me secretly. 'Poorly, poorly Karl!' she sayt. 'Nopoty loaf you, pot I will not exchange you for somepoty in ze worlt, One zing your

Mutter pegs you, to rememper,' sayt she to me, 'learn vell, ant be efer one honest man; zen Got will not forsake you.' Ant I triet so to become. Ven my fourteen year hat expiret, ant me coult partake of ze Holy Sopper, my *Mutter* sayt to my *Vater*, 'Karl is one pig poy now, Kustaf. Vat shall we do wis him?' Ant Papa sayt, 'Me ton't know.' Zen Mamma sayt, 'Let us give him to town at Mister Schultzen's, and he may pe a *Schumacher*,' ant my *Vater* sayt, 'Goot!' Six year ant seven mons livet I in town wis ze Mister Shoemaker, ant he loaft me. He sayt, 'Karl are one goot vorkman, ant shall soon become my *Geselle*.' Pot—man makes ze proposition, ant Got ze deposition. In ze year 1796 one conscription took place, ant each which vas serviceable, from ze eighteens to ze twenty-first year, hat to go to town.

"My *Fater* and my broser Johann come to town, ant ve go togezer to throw ze lot for which shoult pe *Soldat*. Johann drew ze fatal nomper, and me vas not necessary to pe *Soldat*. Ant Papa sayt, 'I have only vun son, ant wis him I must now separate!'

"Den I take his hant, ant says, 'Why say you so, Papa? Come wis me, ant I will say you somesing.' Ant Papa come, ant we seat togezer at ze publics-house, ant me sayt, 'Vaiter, give us one *Bierkrug*,' ant he gives us one. We trink altogezer, and broser Johann also trink. 'Papa,' sayt me, 'ton't say zat you have only one son, ant wis it you must separate, My heart was breaking ven you say sis. Broser Johann must not serve; *me* shall pe *Soldat*. Karl is for nopoty necessary, and Karl shall pe *Soldat*.'

"'You is one honest man, Karl,' sayt Papa, ant kiss me. Ant me was *Soldat*."

IX.
Continuation of Karl's Narrative

"Zat was a terrible time, Nicolinka," continued Karl Ivanitch, "ze time of Napoleon. He vanted to conquer Germany, ant we protected our *Vaterland* to ze last trop of plot. Me vere at Ulm, me vere at Austerlitz, me vere at Wagram."

"Did you really fight?" I asked with a gaze of astonishment "Did you really kill anybody?"

Karl instantly reassured me on this point,

"Vonce one French grenadier was left behint, ant fell to ze grount. I sprang forvarts wis my gon, ant vere about to kill him, *aber der Franzose warf sein Gewehr hin und rief*, 'Pardon'—ant I let him loose.

"At Wagram, Napoleon cut us open, ant surrountet us in such a way as zere vas no helping. Sree days hat we no provisions, ant stoot in ze vater op to ze knees. Ze evil Napoleon neiser let us go loose nor catchet us.

"On ze fours day zey took us prisoners—zank Got! ant sent us to one fortress. Upon me vas one blue trousers, uniforms of very goot clos, fifteen of *Thalers*, ant one silver clock which my *Vater* hat given me, Ze Frans *Soldaten* took from me everysing. For my happiness zere vas sree tucats on me which my Mamma hat sewn in my shirt of flannel. Nopoty fount zem.

"I liket not long to stay in ze fortresses, ant resoluted to ron away. Von day, von pig holitay, says I to the sergeant which hat to look after us, 'Mister Sergeant, to-day is a pig holitay, ant me vants to celeprate it. Pring here, if you please, two pottle Mateira, ant we shall trink zem wis each oser.' Ant ze sergeant says, 'Goot!' Ven ze sergeant pring ze Mateira ant we trink it out to ze last trop, I taket his hant ant says,

'Mister Sergeant, perhaps you have still one *Vater* and one *Mutter*?' He says, 'So I have, Mister Mayer.' 'My *Vater* ant *Mutter* not seen me eight year,' I goes on to him, 'ant zey know not if I am yet alive or if my bones be reposing in ze grave. Oh, Mister Sergeant, I have two tucats which is in my shirt of flannel. Take zem, ant let me loose! You will pe my penefactor, ant my *Mutter* will be praying for you all her life to ze Almighty Got!'

"Ze sergeant emptiet his glass of Mateira, ant says, 'Mister Mayer, I loaf and pity you very much, pot you is one prisoner, ant I one *soldat*.' So I take his hant ant says, 'Mister Sergeant!'

"Ant ze sergeant says, 'You is one poor man, ant I will not take your money, pot I will help you. Ven I go to sleep, puy one pail of pranty for ze *Soldaten*, ant zey will sleep. Me will not look after you.' Sis was one goot man. I puyet ze pail of pranty, ant ven ze *Soldaten* was trunken me tresset in one olt coat, ant gang in silence out of ze doon.

"I go to ze wall, ant will leap down, pot zere is vater pelow, ant I will not spoil my last tressing, so I go to ze gate.

"Ze sentry go up and town wis one gon, ant look at me. 'Who goes zere?' ant I was silent. 'Who goes zere ze second time?' ant I was silent. 'Who goes zere ze third time?' ant I ron away, I sprang in ze vater, climp op to ze oser site, ant walk on.

"Ze entire night I ron on ze vay, pot ven taylight came I was afrait zat zey woult catch me, ant I hit myself in ze high corn. Zere I kneelet town, zanket ze *Vater* in Heaven for my safety, ant fall asleep wis a tranquil feeling.

"I wakenet op in ze evening, ant gang furser. At once one large German carriage, wis two raven-black horse, came alongside me. In ze carriage sit one well-tresset man, smoking pipe, ant look at me. I go slowly, so zat ze carriage shall have time to pass me, pot I go slowly, ant ze carriage go slowly, ant ze man look at me. I go quick, ant ze carriage go quick, ant ze man stop its two horses, ant look at me. 'Young man,' says he, 'where go you so late?' I says, 'I go to Frankfort.' 'Sit in ze carriage—zere is room enough, ant I will trag you,' he says. 'Bot why have you nosing about you? Your boots is dirty, ant your beart not shaven.' I seated wis him, ant says, '*Ich bin* one poor man, ant I would like to pusy myself wis somesing in a manufactory. My tressing is dirty because I fell in ze mud on ze roat.'

"'You tell me ontruse, young man,' says he. 'Ze roat is kvite dry now.' I was silent. 'Tell me ze *whole* truse,' goes on ze goot man—'who you are, ant vere you go to? I like your face, ant ven you is one honest man, so I will help you.' Ant I tell all.

"'Goot, young man!' he says. 'Come to my manufactory of rope, ant I will give you work ant tress ant money, ant you can live wis os.' I says, 'Goot!'

"I go to ze manufactory of rope, ant ze goot man says to his voman, 'Here is one yong man who defented his *Vaterland*, ant ron away from prisons. He has not house nor tresses nor preat. He will live wis os. Give him clean linen, ant norish him.'

"I livet one ant a half year in ze manufactory of rope, ant my lantlort loaft me so much zat he would not let me loose. Ant I felt very goot.

"I were zen handsome man—yong, of pig stature, with blue eyes and *römische* nose—ant Missis L— (I like not to say her name—she was ze voman of my lantlort) was yong ant handsome laty. Ant she fell in loaf wis mc."

Here Karl Ivanitch made a long pause, lowered his kindly blue eyes, shook his head quietly, and smiled as people always do under the influence of a pleasing recollection.

"Yes," he resumed as he leant back in his arm-chair and adjusted his dressing-gown, "I have experiencet many sings in my life, pot zere is my witness,"—here he pointed to an image of the Saviour, embroidered on wool, which was hanging over his bed—"zat nopoty in ze worlt can say zat Karl Ivanitch has been one dishonest man, I would not repay black ingratitude for ze goot which Mister L— dit me, ant I resoluted to ron away. So in ze evening, ven all were asleep, I writet one letter to my lantlort, ant laid it on ze table in his room. Zen I taket my tresses, tree *Thaler* of money, ant go mysteriously into ze street. Nopoty have seen me, ant I go on ze roat."

X.
Conclusion of Karl's Narrative

"I had not seen my Mamma for nine year, ant I know not whether she lived or whether her bones had long since lain in ze dark grave. Ven I come to my own country and go to ze town I ask, 'Where live Kustaf Mayer who was farmer to ze Count von Zomerblat?' ant zey answer me, '*Graf* Zomerblat is deat, ant Kustaf Mayer live now in ze pig street, ant keep a public-house.' So I tress in my new waistcoat and one noble coat which ze manufacturist presented me, arranged my hairs nice, ant go to ze public-house of my Papa. Sister Mariechen vas sitting on a pench, and she ask me what I want. I says, 'Might I trink one glass of pranty?' ant she says, '*Vater*, here is a yong man who wish to trink one glass of pranty.' Ant Papa says, 'Give him ze glass.' I set to ze table, trink my glass of pranty, smoke my pipe, ant look at Papa, Mariechen, ant Johann (who also come into ze shop). In ze conversation Papa says, 'You know, perhaps, yong man, where stants our army?' and I say, 'I myself am come from ze army, ant it stants now at Wien.' 'Our son,' says Papa, 'is a *Soldat*, ant now is it nine years since he wrote never one wort, and we know not whether he is alive or dead. My voman cry continually for him.' I still fumigate the pipe, ant say, 'What was your son's name, and where servet he? Perhaps I may know him.' 'His name was Karl Mayer, ant he servet in ze Austrian Jägers.' 'He were of pig stature, ant a handsome man like yourself,' puts in Mariechen. I say, 'I know your Karl.' 'Amalia,' exclaimet my *Vater*. 'Come here! Here is yong man which knows our Karl!'—ant my dear *Mutter* comes out from a back door. I knew her directly. 'You know our Karl?' says she, ant looks at me, ant, white all over, trembles. 'Yes, I haf seen him,' I says, without ze corage to look at her, for my heart did almost burst. 'My Karl is alive?' she cry. 'Zen tank Got! Vere is he, my Karl? I woult die in peace if I coult see him once more—my darling son! Bot Got will not haf it so.' Then she cried, and I coult no longer stant it. 'Darling Mamma!' I say, 'I am your son, I am your Karl!'—and she fell into my arms."

Karl Ivanitch covered his eyes, and his lips were quivering.

"'*Mutter,' sagte ich, 'ich bin ihr Sohn, ich bin ihr Karl!'—und sie stürtzte mir in die Arme!*'" he repeated, recovering a little and wiping the tears from his eyes.

"Bot Got did not wish me to finish my tays in my own town. I were pursuet by fate. I livet in my own town only sree mons. One Suntay I sit in a coffee-house, ant trinket one pint of *Pier*, ant fumigated my pipe, ant speaket wis some frients of *Politik*, of ze Emperor Franz, of Napoleon, of ze war—ant anypoty might say his opinion. But next to us sits a strange chentleman in a grey *Uberrock*, who trink coffee, fumigate the pipe, ant says nosing. Ven the night watchman shoutet ten o'clock I taket my hat, paid ze money, and go home. At ze middle of ze night some one knock at ze door. I rise ant says, 'Who is zere?' 'Open!' says someone. I shout again, 'First say who is zere, ant I will open.' 'Open in the name of the law!' say the someone behint the door. I now do so. Two *Soldaten* wis gons stant at ze door, ant into ze room steps ze man in ze grey *Uberrock*, who had sat with us in ze coffeehouse. He were *Spion!* 'Come wis me,' says ze *Spion*, 'Very goot!' say I. I dresset myself in boots, trousers, ant coat, ant go srough ze room. Ven I come to ze wall where my gon hangs I take it, ant says, 'You are a *Spion*, so defent you!' I give one stroke left, one right, ant one on ze head. Ze *Spion* lay precipitated on ze floor! Zen I taket my cloak-bag ant money, ant jompet out of ze vintow. I vent to Ems, where I was acquainted wis one General Sasin, who loaft me, givet me a passport from ze Embassy, ant taket me to Russland to learn his chiltren. Ven General Sasin tiet, your Mamma callet for me, ant says, 'Karl Ivanitch, I gif you my children. Loaf them, ant I will never leave you, ant will take care for your olt age.' Now is she teat, ant all is forgotten! For my twenty year full of service I most now go into ze street ant seek for a try crust of preat for my olt age! Got sees all sis, ant knows all sis. His holy will be done! Only-only, I yearn for you, my children!"—and Karl drew me to him, and kissed me on the forehead.

XI.
One Mark Only

The year of mourning over, Grandmamma recovered a little from her grief, and once more took to receiving occasional guests, especially children of the same age as ourselves.

On the 13th of December—Lubotshka's birthday—the Princess Kornakoff and her daughters, with Madame Valakhin, Sonetchka, Ilinka Grap, and the two younger Iwins, arrived at our house before luncheon.

Though we could hear the sounds of talking, laughter, and movements going on in the drawing-room, we could not join the party until our morning lessons were finished. The table of studies in the schoolroom said, "*Lundi, de 2 à 3, maître d'Histoire et de Geographie*," and this infernal *maître d'Histoire* we must await, listen to, and see the back of before we could gain our liberty. Already it was twenty minutes past two, and nothing was to be heard of the tutor, nor yet anything to be seen of him in the street, although I kept looking up and down it with the greatest impatience and with an emphatic longing never to see the *maître* again.

"I believe he is not coming to-day," said Woloda, looking up for a moment from his lesson-book.

"I hope he is not, please the Lord!" I answered, but in a despondent tone. "Yet there he *does* come, I believe, all the same!"

"Not he! Why, that is a *gentleman*," said Woloda, likewise looking out of the window, "Let us wait till half-past two, and then ask St. Jerome if we may put away our books."

"Yes, and wish them *au revoir*," I added, stretching my arms, with the book clasped in my hands, over my head. Having hitherto idled away my time, I now opened the book at the place where the lesson was to begin, and started to learn it. It was long and difficult, and, moreover, I was in the mood when one's thoughts refuse to be arrested by anything at all. Consequently I made no progress. After our last lesson in history (which always seemed to me a peculiarly arduous and wearisome subject) the history master had complained to St. Jerome of me because only two good marks stood to my credit in the register—a very small total. St. Jerome had then told me that if I failed to gain less than *three* marks at the next lesson I should be severely punished. The next lesson was now imminent, and I confess that I felt a little nervous.

So absorbed, however, did I become in my reading that the sound of goloshes being taken off in the ante-room came upon me almost as a shock. I had just time to look up when there appeared in the doorway the servile and (to me) very disgusting face and form of the master, clad in a blue frockcoat with brass buttons.

Slowly he set down his hat and books and adjusted the folds of his coat (as though such a thing were necessary!), and seated himself in his place.

"Well, gentlemen," he said, rubbing his hands, "let us first of all repeat the general contents of the last lesson: after which I will proceed to narrate the succeeding events of the middle ages."

This meant "Say over the last lesson." While Woloda was answering the master with the entire ease and confidence which come of knowing a subject well, I went aimlessly out on to the landing, and, since I was not allowed to go downstairs, what more natural than that I should involuntarily turn towards the alcove on the landing? Yet before I had time to establish myself in my usual coign of vantage behind the door I found myself pounced upon by Mimi—always the cause of my misfortunes!

"*You* here?" she said, looking severely, first at myself, and then at the maidservants' door, and then at myself again.

I felt thoroughly guilty, firstly, because I was not in the schoolroom, and secondly, because I was in a forbidden place. So I remained silent, and, dropping my head, assumed a touching expression of contrition.

"Indeed, this is *too* bad!" Mimi went on, "What are you doing here?"

Still I said nothing.

"Well, it shall not rest where it is," she added, tapping the banister with her yellow fingers. "I shall inform the Countess."

It was five minutes to three when I re-entered the schoolroom. The master, as though oblivious of my presence or absence, was explaining the new lesson to Woloda. When he had finished doing this, and had put his books together (while Woloda went into the other room to fetch his ticket), the comforting idea occurred to me that perhaps the whole thing was over now, and that the master had forgotten me.

But suddenly he turned in my direction with a malicious smile, and said as he rubbed his hands anew, "I hope you have learnt your lesson?"

"Yes," I replied.

"Would you be so kind, then, as to tell me something about St. Louis' Crusade?" he went on, balancing himself on his chair and looking gravely at his feet. "Firstly, tell me something about the reasons which induced the French king to assume the cross" (here he raised his eyebrows and pointed to the inkstand); "then explain to me the general characteristics of the Crusade" (here he made a sweeping gesture with his hand, as though to seize hold of something with it); "and lastly, expound to me the influence of this Crusade upon the European states in general" (drawing the copy books to the left side of the table) "and upon the French state in particular" (drawing one of them to the right, and inclining his head in the same direction).

I swallowed a few times, coughed, bent forward, and was silent. Then, taking a pen from the table, I began to pick it to pieces, yet still said nothing.

"Allow me the pen—I shall want it," said the master. "Well?"

"Louis the-er-Saint was-was-a very good and wise king."

"What?"

"King, He took it into his head to go to Jerusalem, and handed over the reins of government to his mother."

"What was her name?

"B-b-b-lanka."

"What? Belanka?"

I laughed in a rather forced manner.

"Well, is that all you know?" he asked again, smiling.

I had nothing to lose now, so I began chattering the first thing that came into my head. The master remained silent as he gathered together the remains of the pen which I had left strewn about the table, looked gravely past my ear at the wall, and repeated from time to time, "Very well, very well." Though I was conscious that I knew nothing whatever and was expressing myself all wrong, I felt much hurt at the fact that he never either corrected or interrupted me.

"What made him think of going to Jerusalem?" he asked at last, repeating some words of my own.

"Because—because—that is to say—"

My confusion was complete, and I relapsed into silence, I felt that, even if this disgusting history master were to go on putting questions to me, and gazing inquiringly into my face, for a year, I should never be able to enunciate another syllable. After staring at me for some three minutes, he suddenly assumed a mournful cast of countenance, and said in an agitated voice to Woloda (who was just re-entering the room):

"Allow me the register. I will write my remarks."

He opened the book thoughtfully, and in his fine caligraphy marked *five* for Woloda for diligence, and the same for good behaviour. Then, resting his pen on the line where my report was to go, he looked at me and reflected. Suddenly his hand made a decisive movement and, behold, against my name stood a clearly-marked *one*, with a full stop after it! Another movement and in the behaviour column there stood another *one* and another full stop! Quietly closing the book, the master then rose, and moved towards the door as though unconscious of my look of entreaty, despair, and reproach.

"Michael Lavionitch!" I said.

"No!" he replied, as though knowing beforehand what I was about to say. "It is impossible for you to learn in that way. I am not going to earn my money for nothing."

He put on his goloshes and cloak, and then slowly tied a scarf about his neck. To think that he could care about such trifles after what had just happened to me! To him it was all a mere stroke of the pen, but to me it meant the direst misfortune.

"Is the lesson over?" asked St. Jerome, entering.

"Yes."

"And was the master pleased with you?"

"Yes."

"How many marks did he give you?"

"Five."

"And to Nicholas?"

I was silent.

"I think four," said Woloda. His idea was to save me for at least today. If punishment there must be, it need not be awarded while we had guests.

"Voyons, Messieurs!" (St. Jerome was forever saying "Voyons!") *"Faites votre toilette, et descendons."*

XII.
The Key

We had hardly descended and greeted our guests when luncheon was announced. Papa was in the highest of spirits since for some time past he had been winning. He had presented Lubotshka with a silver tea service, and suddenly remembered, after luncheon, that he had forgotten a box of bonbons which she was to have too.

"Why send a servant for it? *You* had better go, Koko," he said to me jestingly. "The keys are in the tray on the table, you know. Take them, and with the largest one open the second drawer on the right. There you will find the box of bonbons. Bring it here."

"Shall I get you some cigars as well?" said I, knowing that he always smoked after luncheon.

"Yes, do; but don't touch anything else."

I found the keys, and was about to carry out my orders, when I was seized with a desire to know what the smallest of the keys on the bunch belonged to.

On the table I saw, among many other things, a padlocked portfolio, and at once felt curious to see if *that* was what the key fitted. My experiment was crowned with success. The portfolio opened and disclosed a number of papers. Curiosity so strongly urged me also to ascertain what those papers contained that the voice of conscience was stilled, and I began to read their contents. . . .

My childish feeling of unlimited respect for my elders, especially for Papa, was so strong within me that my intellect involuntarily refused to draw any conclusions from what I had seen. I felt that Papa was living in a sphere completely apart from, incomprehensible by, and unattainable for, me, as well as one that was in every way excellent, and that any attempt on my part to criticise the secrets of his life would constitute something like sacrilege.

For this reason, the discovery which I made from Papa's portfolio left no clear impression upon my mind, but only a dim consciousness that I had done wrong. I felt ashamed and confused.

The feeling made me eager to shut the portfolio again as quickly as possible, but it seemed as though on this unlucky day I was destined to experience every possible kind of adversity. I put the key back into the padlock and turned it round, but not in the right direction. Thinking that the portfolio was now locked, I pulled at the key and, oh horror! found my hand come away with only the top half of the key in it! In vain did I try to put the two halves together, and to extract the portion that was sticking in the padlock. At last I had to resign myself to the dreadful thought that I had committed a new crime—one which would be discovered to-day as soon as ever Papa returned to his study! First of all, Mimi's accusation on the staircase, and then that one mark, and then this key! Nothing worse could happen now. This very evening I should be assailed successively by Grandmamma (because of Mimi's denunciation), by St. Jerome (because of the solitary mark), and by Papa (because of the matter of this key)—yes, all in one evening!

"What on earth is to become of me? What have I done?" I exclaimed as I paced the soft carpet. "Well," I went on with sudden determination, "what *must* come, *must*—that's all;" and, taking up the bonbons and the cigars, I ran back to the other part of the house.

The fatalistic formula with which I had concluded (and which was one that I often heard Nicola utter during my childhood) always produced in me, at the more difficult crises of my life, a momentarily soothing, beneficial effect. Consequently, when I re-entered the drawing-room, I was in a rather excited, unnatural mood, yet one that was perfectly cheerful.

XIII.
The Traitress

After luncheon we began to play at round games, in which I took a lively part. While indulging in "cat and mouse", I happened to cannon rather awkwardly against the Kornakoffs' governess, who was playing with us, and, stepping on her dress, tore a large hole in it. Seeing that the girls—particularly Sonetchka—were anything but displeased at the spectacle of the governess angrily departing to the maidservants' room to have her dress mended, I resolved to procure them the satisfaction a second time. Accordingly, in pursuance of this amiable resolution, I waited until my victim returned, and then began to gallop madly round her, until a favourable moment occurred for once more planting my heel upon her dress and reopening the rent. Sonetchka and the young princesses had much ado to restrain their laughter, which excited my conceit the more, but St. Jerome, who had probably divined my tricks, came up to me with the frown which I could never abide in him, and said that, since I seemed disposed to mischief, he would have to send me away if I did not moderate my behaviour.

However, I was in the desperate position of a person who, having staked more than he has in his pocket, and feeling that he can never make up his account, continues to plunge on unlucky cards—not because he hopes to regain his losses, but because it will not do for him to stop and consider. So, I merely laughed in an impudent fashion and flung away from my monitor.

After "cat and mouse", another game followed in which the gentlemen sit on one row of chairs and the ladies on another, and choose each other for partners. The youngest princess always chose the younger Iwin, Katenka either Woloda or Ilinka, and Sonetchka Seriosha—nor, to my extreme astonishment, did Sonetchka seem at all embarrassed when her cavalier went and sat down beside her. On the contrary, she only laughed her sweet, musical laugh, and made a sign with her head that he had chosen right. Since nobody chose *me*, I always had the mortification of finding myself left over, and of hearing them say, "Who has been left out? Oh, Nicolinka. Well, *do* take him, somebody." Consequently, whenever it came to my turn to guess who had chosen me, I had to go either to my sister or to one of the ugly elder princesses. Sonetchka seemed so absorbed in Seriosha that in her eyes I clearly existed no longer. I do not quite know why I called her "the traitress" in my thoughts, since she had never promised to choose me instead of Seriosha, but, for all that, I felt convinced that she was treating me in a very abominable fashion. After the game was finished, I actually saw "the traitress" (from whom I nevertheless could not withdraw my eyes) go with Seriosha and Katenka into a corner, and engage in secret confabulation. Stealing softly round the piano which masked the conclave, I beheld the following:

Katenka was holding up a pocket-handkerchief by two of its corners, so as to form a screen for the heads of her two companions. "No, you have lost! You must pay the forfeit!" cried Seriosha at that moment, and Sonetchka, who was standing in front of him, blushed like a criminal as she replied, "No, I have *not* lost! *Have* I, Mademoiselle Katherine?" "Well, I must speak the truth," answered Katenka, "and say that you *have* lost, my dear." Scarcely had she spoken the words when Seriosha embraced Sonetchka, and kissed her right on her rosy lips! And Sonetchka smiled as though it were nothing, but merely something very pleasant!

Horrors! The artful "traitress!"

XIV.
The Retribution

Instantly, I began to feel a strong contempt for the female sex in general and Sonetchka in particular. I began to think that there was nothing at all amusing in these games—that they were only fit for girls, and felt as though I should like to make a great noise, or to do something of such extraordinary boldness that every one would be forced to admire it. The opportunity soon arrived. St. Jerome said something to Mimi, and then left the room, I could hear his footsteps ascending the staircase, and then passing across the schoolroom, and the idea occurred to me that Mimi must have told him her story about my being found on the landing, and thereupon he had gone to look at the register. (In those days, it must be remembered, I believed that St. Jerome's whole aim in life was to annoy me.) Some where I have read that, not infrequently, children of from twelve to fourteen years of age—that is to say, children just passing from childhood to adolescence—are addicted to incendiarism, or even to murder. As I look back upon my childhood, and particularly upon the mood in which I was on that (for myself) most unlucky day, I can quite understand the possibility of such terrible crimes being committed by children without any real aim in view—without any real wish to do wrong, but merely out of curiosity or under the influence of an unconscious necessity for action. There are moments when the human being sees the future in such lurid colours that he shrinks from fixing his mental eye upon it, puts a check upon all his intellectual activity, and tries to feel convinced that the future will never be, and that the past has never been. At such moments—moments when thought does not shrink from manifestations of will, and the carnal instincts alone constitute the springs of life—I can understand that want of experience (which is a particularly predisposing factor in this connection) might very possibly lead a child, aye, without fear or hesitation, but rather with a smile of curiosity on its face, to set fire to the house in which its parents and brothers and sisters (beings whom it tenderly loves) are lying asleep. It would be under the same influence of momentary absence of thought—almost absence of mind—that a peasant boy of seventeen might catch sight of the edge of a newly-sharpened axe reposing near the bench on which his aged father was lying asleep, face downwards, and suddenly raise the implement in order to observe with unconscious curiosity how the blood would come spurting out upon the floor if he made a wound in the sleeper's neck. It is under the same influence—the same absence of thought, the same instinctive curiosity—that a man finds delight in standing on the brink of an abyss and thinking to himself, "How if I were to throw myself down?" or in holding to his brow a loaded pistol and wondering, "What if I were to pull the trigger?" or in feeling, when he catches sight of some universally respected personage, that he would like to go up to him, pull his nose hard, and say, "How do you do, old boy?"

Under the spell, then, of this instinctive agitation and lack of reflection I was moved to put out my tongue, and to say that I would not move, when St. Jerome came down and told me that I had behaved so badly that day, as well as done my lessons so ill, that I had no right to be where I was, and must go upstairs directly.

At first, from astonishment and anger, he could not utter a word.

"*C'est bien!*" he exclaimed eventually as he darted towards me. "Several times have I promised to punish you, and you have been saved from it by your Grandmamma, but now I see that nothing but the cane will teach you obedience, and you shall therefore taste it."

This was said loud enough for every one to hear. The blood rushed to my heart with such vehemence that I could feel that organ beating violently—could feel the colour rising to my cheeks and my lips trembling. Probably I looked horrible at that moment, for, avoiding my eye, St. Jerome stepped forward and caught me by the hand. Hardly feeling his touch, I pulled away my hand in blind fury, and with all my childish might struck him.

"What are you doing?" said Woloda, who had seen my behaviour, and now approached me in alarm and astonishment.

"Let me alone!" I exclaimed, the tears flowing fast. "Not a single one of you loves me or understands how miserable I am! You are all of you odious and disgusting!" I added bluntly, turning to the company at large.

At this moment St. Jerome—his face pale, but determined—approached me again, and, with a movement too quick to admit of any defence, seized my hands as with a pair of tongs, and dragged me away. My head swam with excitement, and I can only remember that, so long as I had strength to do it, I fought with head and legs; that my nose several times collided with a pair of knees; that my teeth tore some one's coat; that all around me I could hear the shuffling of feet; and that I could smell dust and the scent of violets with which St. Jerome used to perfume himself.

Five minutes later the door of the store-room closed behind me.

"Basil," said a triumphant but detestable voice, "bring me the cane."

XV.
Dreams

Could I at that moment have supposed that I should ever live to survive the misfortunes of that day, or that there would ever come a time when I should be able to look back upon those misfortunes composedly?

As I sat there thinking over what I had done, I could not imagine what the matter had been with me. I only felt with despair that I was for ever lost.

At first the most profound stillness reigned around me—at least, so it appeared to me as compared with the violent internal emotion which I had been experiencing; but by and by I began to distinguish various sounds. Basil brought something downstairs which he laid upon a chest outside. It sounded like a broom-stick. Below me I could hear St. Jerome's grumbling voice (probably he was speaking of me), and then children's voices and laughter and footsteps; until in a few moments everything seemed to have regained its normal course in the house, as though nobody knew or cared to know that here was I sitting alone in the dark store-room!

I did not cry, but something lay heavy, like a stone, upon my heart. Ideas and pictures passed with extraordinary rapidity before my troubled imagination, yet through their fantastic sequence broke continually the remembrance of the misfortune which had befallen me as I once again plunged into an interminable labyrinth of conjectures as to the punishment, the fate, and the despair that were awaiting me. The thought occurred to me that there must be some reason for the general dislike—even contempt—which I fancied to be felt for me by others. I was firmly convinced that every one, from Grandmamma down to the coachman Philip, despised me, and found pleasure in my sufferings.

Next an idea struck me that perhaps I was not the son of my father and mother at all, nor Woloda's brother, but only some unfortunate orphan who had been adopted by them out of compassion, and this absurd notion not only afforded me a certain melancholy consolation, but seemed to me quite probable. I found it comforting to think that I was unhappy, not through my own fault, but because I was fated to be so from my birth, and conceived that my destiny was very much like poor Karl Ivanitch's.

"Why conceal the secret any longer, now that I have discovered it?" I reflected. "To-morrow I will go to Papa and say to him, 'It is in vain for you to try and conceal from me the mystery of my birth. I know it already.' And he will answer me, 'What else could I do, my good fellow? Sooner or later you would have had to know that you are not my son, but were adopted as such. Nevertheless, so long as you remain worthy of my love, I will never cast you out.' Then I shall say, 'Papa, though I have no right to call you by that name, and am now doing so for the last time, I have always loved you, and shall always retain that love. At the same time, while I can never forget that you have been my benefactor, I cannot remain longer in your house. Nobody here loves me, and St. Jerome has wrought my ruin. Either he or I must go forth, since I cannot answer for myself. I hate the man so that I could do anything—I could even kill him.' Papa will begin to entreat me, but I shall make a gesture, and say, 'No, no, my friend and benefactor! We cannot live together. Let me go'—and for the last time I shall embrace him, and say in French, '*O mon père, O mon bienfaiteur, donne moi, pour la dernière fois, ta bénédiction, et que la volonté de Dieu soit faite!*'"

I sobbed bitterly at these thoughts as I sat on a trunk in that dark storeroom. Then, suddenly recollecting the shameful punishment which was awaiting me, I would find myself back again in actuality, and the dreams had fled. Soon, again, I began to fancy myself far away from the house and alone in the world. I enter a hussar regiment and go to war. Surrounded by the foe on every side, I wave my sword, and kill one of them and wound another—then a third,—then a fourth. At last, exhausted with loss of blood and fatigue, I fall to the ground and cry, "Victory!" The general comes to look for me, asking, "Where is our saviour?" whereupon I am pointed out to him. He embraces me, and, in his turn, exclaims with tears of joy, "Victory!" I recover and, with my arm in a black sling, go to walk on the boulevards. I am a general now. I meet the Emperor, who asks, "Who is this young man who has been wounded?" He is told that it is the famous hero Nicolas; whereupon he approaches me and says, "My thanks to you! Whatsoever you may ask for, I will grant it." To this I bow respectfully, and, leaning on my sword, reply, "I am happy, most august Emperor, that I have been able to shed my blood for my country. I would gladly have died for it. Yet, since you are so generous as to grant any wish of mine, I venture to ask of you permission to annihilate my enemy, the foreigner St. Jerome" And then I step fiercely before St. Jerome and say, "*you* were the cause of all my fortunes! Down now on your knees!"

Unfortunately this recalled to my mind the fact that at any moment the *real* St. Jerome might be entering with the cane; so that once more I saw myself, not a general and the saviour of my country, but an unhappy, pitiful creature.

Then the idea of God occurred to me, and I asked Him boldly why He had punished me thus, seeing that I had never forgotten to say my prayers, either morning or evening. Indeed, I can positively declare that it was during that hour in the store-room that I took the first step towards the religious doubt which afterwards assailed me during my youth (not that mere misfortune could arouse me to infidelity and murmuring, but that, at moments of utter contrition and solitude, the idea of the injustice of Providence took root in me as readily as bad seed takes root in land well soaked with rain). Also, I imagined that I was going to die there and then, and drew vivid pictures of St. Jerome's astonishment when he entered the store-room and found a corpse there instead of myself! Likewise, recollecting what Natalia Savishna had told me of the forty days during which the souls of the departed must hover around their earthly home, I imagined myself flying through the rooms of Grandmamma's house, and seeing Lubotshka's bitter tears, and hearing Grandmamma's lamentations, and listening to Papa and St. Jerome talking together. "He was a fine boy," Papa would say with tears in his eyes. "Yes," St. Jerome would reply, "but a sad scapegrace and good-for-nothing." "But you should respect the dead," would expostulate Papa. "*You* were the cause of his death; *you* frightened him until he could no longer bear the thought of the humiliation which you were about to inflict upon him. Away from me, criminal!" Upon that St.

Jerome would fall upon his knees and implore forgiveness, and when the forty days were ended my soul would fly to Heaven, and see there something wonderfully beautiful, white, and transparent, and know that it was Mamma.

And that something would embrace and caress me. Yet, all at once, I should feel troubled, and not know her. "If it be you," I should say to her, "show yourself more distinctly, so that I may embrace you in return." And her voice would answer me, "Do you not feel happy thus?" and I should reply, "Yes, I do, but you cannot *really* caress me, and I cannot *really* kiss your hand like this." "But it is not necessary," she would say. "There can be happiness here without that,"—and I should feel that it was so, and we should ascend together, ever higher and higher, until—Suddenly I feel as though I am being thrown down again, and find myself sitting on the trunk in the dark store-room (my cheeks wet with tears and my thoughts in a mist), yet still repeating the words, "Let us ascend together, higher and higher." Indeed, it was a long, long while before I could remember where I was, for at that moment my mind's eye saw only a dark, dreadful, illimitable void. I tried to renew the happy, consoling dream which had been thus interrupted by the return to reality, but, to my surprise, I found that, as soon as ever I attempted to re-enter former dreams, their continuation became impossible, while—which astonished me even more—they no longer gave me pleasure.

XVI.

"Keep On Grinding, And You'll Have Flour"

I passed the night in the store-room, and nothing further happened, except that on the following morning—a Sunday—I was removed to a small chamber adjoining the schoolroom, and once more shut up. I began to hope that my punishment was going to be limited to confinement, and found my thoughts growing calmer under the influence of a sound, soft sleep, the clear sunlight playing upon the frost crystals of the windowpanes, and the familiar noises in the street.

Nevertheless, solitude gradually became intolerable. I wanted to move about, and to communicate to some one all that was lying upon my heart, but not a living creature was near me. The position was the more unpleasant because, willy-nilly, I could hear St. Jerome walking about in his room, and softly whistling some hackneyed tune. Somehow, I felt convinced that he was whistling not because he wanted to, but because he knew it annoyed me.

At two o'clock, he and Woloda departed downstairs, and Nicola brought me up some luncheon. When I told him what I had done and what was awaiting me he said:

"Pshaw, sir! Don't be alarmed. 'Keep on grinding, and you'll have flour.'"

Although this expression (which also in later days has more than once helped me to preserve my firmness of mind) brought me a little comfort, the fact that I received, not bread and water only, but a whole luncheon, and even dessert, gave me much to think about. If they had sent me no dessert, it would have meant that my punishment was to be limited to confinement; whereas it was now evident that I was looked upon as not yet punished—that I was only being kept away from the others, as an evil-doer, until the due time of punishment. While I was still debating the question, the key of my prison turned, and St. Jerome entered with a severe, official air.

"Come down and see your Grandmamma," he said without looking at me.

I should have liked first to have brushed my jacket, since it was covered with dust, but St. Jerome said that that was quite unnecessary, since I was in such a deplorable moral condition that my exterior was not worth considering. As he led me through the salon, Katenka, Lubotshka, and Woloda looked at me with much the same expression as we were wont to look at the convicts who on certain days filed past my grandmother's house. Likewise, when I approached Grandmamma's arm-chair to kiss her hand, she withdrew it, and thrust it under her mantilla.

"Well, my dear," she began after a long pause, during which she regarded me from head to foot with the kind of expression which makes one uncertain where to look or what to do, "I must say that you seem to value my love very highly, and afford me great consolation." Then she went on, with an emphasis on each word, "Monsieur St. Jerome, who, at my request, undertook your education, says that he can no longer remain in the house. And why? Simply because of you." Another pause ensued. Presently she continued in a tone which clearly showed that her speech had been prepared beforehand, "I had hoped that you would be grateful for all his care, and for all the trouble that he has taken with you, that you would have appreciated his services; but you—you baby, you silly boy!—you actually dare to raise your hand against him! Very well, very good. I am beginning to think that you cannot understand kind treatment, but require to be treated in a very different and humiliating fashion. Go now directly and beg his pardon," she added in a stern and peremptory tone as she pointed to St. Jerome, "Do you hear me?"

I followed the direction of her finger with my eye, but on that member alighting upon St. Jerome's coat, I turned my head away, and once more felt my heart beating violently as I remained where I was.

"What? Did you not hear me when I told you what to do?"

I was trembling all over, but I would not stir.

"Koko," went on my grandmother, probably divining my inward sufferings, "Koko," she repeated in a voice tender rather than harsh, "is this you?"

"Grandmamma, I cannot beg his pardon for—" and I stopped suddenly, for I felt the next word refuse to come for the tears that were choking me.

"But I ordered you, I begged of you, to do so. What is the matter with you?"

"I-I-I will not—I cannot!" I gasped, and the tears, long pent up and accumulated in my breast, burst forth like a stream which breaks its dikes and goes flowing madly over the country.

"C'est ainsi que vous obéissez à votre seconde mère, c'est ainsi que vous reconnaissez ses bontés!" remarked St. Jerome quietly, *"A genoux!"*

"Good God! If *she* had seen this!" exclaimed Grandmamma, turning from me and wiping away her tears. "If she had seen this! It may be all for the best, yet she could never have survived such grief—never!" and Grandmamma wept more and more. I too wept, but it never occurred to me to ask for pardon.

"Tranquillisez-vous au nom du ciel, Madame la Comtesse," said St. Jerome, but Grandmamma heard him not. She covered her face with her hands, and her sobs soon passed to hiccups and hysteria. Mimi and Gasha came running in with frightened faces, salts and spirits were applied, and the whole house was soon in a ferment.

"You may feel pleased at your work," said St. Jerome to me as he led me from the room.

"Good God! What have I done?" I thought to myself. "What a terribly bad boy I am!"

As soon as St. Jerome, bidding me go into his room, had returned to Grandmamma, I, all unconscious of what I was doing, ran down the grand staircase leading to the front door. Whether I intended to drown myself, or whether merely to run away from home, I do not remember. I only know that I went blindly on, my face covered with my hands that I might see nothing.

"Where are you going to?" asked a well-known voice. "I want you, my boy."

I would have passed on, but Papa caught hold of me, and said sternly:

"Come here, you impudent rascal. How could you dare to do such a thing as to touch the portfolio in my study?" he went on as he dragged me into his room. "Oh! you are silent, eh?" and he pulled my ear.

"Yes, I *was* naughty," I said. "I don't know myself what came over me then."

"So you don't know what came over you—you don't know, you don't know?" he repeated as he pulled my ear harder and harder. "Will you go and put your nose where you ought not to again—will you, will you?"

Although my ear was in great pain, I did not cry, but, on the contrary, felt a sort of morally pleasing sensation. No sooner did he let go of my ear than I seized his hand and covered it with tears and kisses.

"Please whip me!" I cried, sobbing. "Please hurt me the more and more, for I am a wretched, bad, miserable boy!"

"Why, what on earth is the matter with you?" he said, giving me a slight push from him.

"No, I will not go away!" I continued, seizing his coat. "Every one else hates me—I know that, but do *you* listen to me and protect me, or else send me away altogether. I cannot live with *him*. He tries to humiliate me—he tells me to kneel before him, and wants to strike me. I can't stand it. I'm not a baby. I can't stand it—I shall die, I shall kill myself. *He* told Grandmamma that I was naughty, and now she is ill—she will die through me. It is all his fault. Please let me—W-why should-he-torment me?"

The tears choked my further speech. I sat down on the sofa, and, with my head buried on Papa's knees, sobbed until I thought I should die of grief.

"Come, come! Why are you such a water-pump?" said Papa compassionately, as he stooped over me.

"He is such a bully! He is murdering me! I shall die! Nobody loves me at all!" I gasped almost inaudibly, and went into convulsions.

Papa lifted me up, and carried me to my bedroom, where I fell asleep.

When I awoke it was late. Only a solitary candle burned in the room, while beside the bed there were seated Mimi, Lubotshka, and our doctor. In their faces I could discern anxiety for my health, so, although I felt so well after my twelve-hours' sleep that I could have got up directly, I thought it best to let them continue thinking that I was unwell.

XVII.
Hatred

Yes, it was the real feeling of hatred that was mine now—not the hatred of which one reads in novels, and in the existence of which I do not believe—the hatred which finds satisfaction in doing harm to a fellow-creature, but the hatred which consists of an unconquerable aversion to a person who may be wholly deserving of your esteem, yet whose very hair, neck, walk, voice, limbs, movements, and everything else are disgusting to you, while all the while an incomprehensible force attracts you towards him, and compels you to follow his slightest acts with anxious attention.

This was the feeling which I cherished for St. Jerome, who had lived with us now for a year and a half.

Judging coolly of the man at this time of day, I find that he was a true Frenchman, but a Frenchman in the better acceptation of the term. He was fairly well educated, and fulfilled his duties to us conscientiously, but he had the peculiar features of fickle egotism, boastfulness, impertinence, and ignorant self-assurance which are common to all his countrymen, as well as entirely opposed to the Russian character.

All this set me against him, Grandmamma had signified to him her dislike for corporal punishment, and therefore he dared not beat us, but he frequently *threatened* us, particularly myself, with the cane, and would utter the word *fouetter* as though it were *fouatter* in an expressive and detestable way which always gave me the idea that to whip me would afford him the greatest possible satisfaction.

I was not in the least afraid of the bodily pain, for I had never experienced it. It was the mere idea that he could beat me that threw me into such paroxysms of wrath and despair.

True, Karl Ivanitch sometimes (in moments of exasperation) had recourse to a ruler or to his braces, but that I can look back upon without anger. Even if he had struck me at the time of which I am now speaking (namely, when I was fourteen years old), I should have submitted quietly to the correction, for I loved him, and had known him all my life, and looked upon him as a member of our family, but St. Jerome was a conceited, opinionated fellow for whom I felt merely the unwilling respect which I entertained for all persons older than myself. Karl Ivanitch was a comical old "Uncle" whom I loved with my whole heart, but who, according to my childish conception of social distinctions, ranked below us, whereas St. Jerome was a well-educated, handsome young dandy who was for showing himself the equal of any one.

Karl Ivanitch had always scolded and punished us coolly, as though he thought it a necessary, but extremely disagreeable, duty. St. Jerome, on the contrary, always liked to emphasise his part as *judge* when correcting us, and clearly did it as much for his own satisfaction as for our good. He loved authority. Nevertheless, I always found his grandiloquent French phrases (which he pronounced with a strong emphasis on all the final syllables) inexpressibly disgusting, whereas Karl, when angry, had never said anything beyond, "What a foolish puppet-comedy it is!" or "You boys are as irritating as Spanish fly!" (which he always called "*Spaniard*" fly). St. Jerome, however, had names for us like "*mauvais sujet*," "*villain*," "*garnement*," and so forth—epithets which greatly offended my self-respect. When Karl Ivanitch ordered us to kneel in the corner with our faces to the wall, the punishment consisted merely in the bodily discomfort of the position, whereas St. Jerome, in such cases, always assumed a haughty air, made a grandiose gesture with his hand, and exclaiming in a pseudo-tragic tone, "*A genoux, mauvais sujet!*" ordered us to kneel with our faces towards him, and to crave his pardon. His punishment consisted in humiliation.

However, on the present occasion the punishment never came, nor was the matter ever referred to again. Yet, I could not forget all that I had gone through—the shame, the fear, and the hatred of those two days. From that time forth, St. Jerome appeared to give me up in despair, and took no further trouble with me, yet I could not bring myself to treat him with indifference. Every time that our eyes met I felt that my look expressed only too plainly my dislike, and, though I tried hard to assume a careless air, he seemed to divine my hypocrisy, until I was forced to blush and turn away.

In short, it was a terrible trial to me to have anything to do with him.

XVIII.
The Maidservants' Room

I began to feel more and more lonely, until my chief solace lay in solitary reflection and observation. Of the favourite subject of my reflections I shall speak in the next chapter. The scene where I indulged in them was, for preference, the maidservants' room, where a plot suitable for a novel was in progress—a plot which touched and engrossed me to the highest degree. The heroine of the romance was, of course, Masha. She was in love with Basil, who had known her before she had become a servant in our house, and who had promised to marry her some day. Unfortunately, fate, which had separated them five years ago, and afterwards reunited them in Grandmamma's abode, next proceeded to interpose an obstacle between them in the shape of Masha's uncle, our man Nicola, who would not hear of his niece marrying that "uneducated and unbearable fellow," as he called Basil. One effect of the obstacle had been to make the otherwise slightly cool and indifferent Basil fall as passionately in love with Masha as it is possible for a man to be who is only a servant and a tailor, wears a red shirt, and has his hair pomaded. Although his methods of expressing his affection were odd (for instance, whenever he met Masha he always endeavoured to inflict upon her some bodily pain, either by pinching her, giving her a slap with his open hand, or squeezing her so hard that she could scarcely breathe), that affection was sincere enough, and he proved it by the fact that, from the moment when Nicola refused him his niece's hand, his grief led him to drinking, and to frequenting taverns, until he proved so unruly that more than once he had to be sent to undergo a humiliating chastisement at the police-station.

Nevertheless, these faults of his and their consequences only served to elevate him in Masha's eyes, and to increase her love for him. Whenever he was in the hands of the police, she would sit crying the whole day, and complain to Gasha of her hard fate (Gasha played an active part in the affairs of these unfortunate lovers). Then, regardless of her uncle's anger and blows, she would stealthily make her way to the police-station, there to visit and console her swain.

Excuse me, reader, for introducing you to such company. Nevertheless, if the cords of love and compassion have not wholly snapped in your soul, you will find, even in that maidservants' room, something which may cause them to vibrate again.

So, whether you please to follow me or not, I will return to the alcove on the staircase whence I was able to observe all that passed in that room. From my post I could see the stove-couch, with, upon it, an iron, an old cap-stand with its peg bent crooked, a wash-tub, and a basin. There, too, was the window, with, in fine disorder before it, a piece of black wax, some fragments of silk, a half-eaten cucumber, a box of sweets, and so on. There, too, was the large table at which *she* used to sit in the pink cotton dress which I admired so much and the blue handkerchief which always caught my attention so. She would be sewing-though interrupting her work at intervals to scratch her head a little, to bite the end of her thread, or to snuff the candle—and I would think to myself: "Why was she not born a lady—she with her blue eyes, beautiful fair hair, and magnificent bust? How splendid she would look if she were sitting in a drawing-room and dressed in a cap with pink ribbons and a silk gown—not one like Mimi's, but one like the gown which I saw the other day on the Tverski Boulevard!" Yes, she would work at the embroidery-frame, and I would sit and look at her in the mirror, and be ready to do whatsoever she wanted—to help her on with her mantle or to hand her food. As for Basil's drunken face and horrid figure in the scanty coat with the red shirt showing beneath it, well, in his every gesture, in his every movement of his back, I seemed always to see signs of the humiliating chastisements which he had undergone.

"Ah, Basil! *Again?*" cried Masha on one occasion as she stuck her needle into the pincushion, but without looking up at the person who was entering.

"What is the good of a man like *him?*" was Basil's first remark.

"Yes. If only he would say something *decisive!* But I am powerless in the matter—I am all at odds and ends, and through his fault, too."

"Will you have some tea?" put in Madesha (another servant).

"No, thank you.—But why does he hate me so, that old thief of an uncle of yours? Why? Is it because of the clothes I wear, or of my height, or of my walk, or what? Well, damn and confound him!" finished Basil, snapping his fingers.

"We must be patient," said Masha, threading her needle.

"You are so—"

"It is my nerves that won't stand it, that's all."

At this moment the door of Grandmamma's room banged, and Gasha's angry voice could be heard as she came up the stairs.

"There!" she muttered with a gesture of her hands. "Try to please people when even they themselves do not know what they want, and it is a cursed life—sheer hard labour, and nothing else! If only a certain thing would happen!—though God forgive me for thinking it!"

"Good evening, Agatha Michaelovna," said Basil, rising to greet her.

"*You* here?" she answered brusquely as she stared at him, "That is not very much to your credit. What do you come here for? Is the maids' room a proper place for men?"

"I wanted to see how you were," said Basil soothingly.

"I shall soon be breathing my last—*that's* how I am!" cried Gasha, still greatly incensed.

Basil laughed.

"Oh, there's nothing to laugh at when I say that I shall soon be dead. But that's how it will be, all the same. Just look at the drunkard! Marry her, would he? The fool! Come, get out of here!" and, with a stamp of her foot on the floor, Gasha retreated to her own room, and banged the door behind her until the window rattled again. For a while she could be heard scolding at everything, flinging dresses and other things about, and pulling the ears of her favourite cat. Then the door opened again, and puss, mewing pitifully, was flung forth by the tail.

"I had better come another time for tea," said Basil in a whisper—"at some better time for our meeting."

"No, no!" put in Madesha. "I'll go and fetch the urn at once."

"I mean to put an end to things soon," went on Basil, seating himself beside Masha as soon as ever Madesha had left the room. "I had much better go straight to the Countess, and say 'so-and-so' or I will throw up my situation and go off into the world. Oh dear, oh dear!"

"And am I to remain here?"

"Ah, there's the difficulty—that's what I feel so badly about, You have been my sweetheart so long, you see. Ah, dear me!"

"Why don't you bring me your shirts to wash, Basil?" asked Masha after a pause, during which she had been inspecting his wrist-bands.

At this moment Grandmamma's bell rang, and Gasha issued from her room again.

"What do you want with her, you impudent fellow?" she cried as she pushed Basil (who had risen at her entrance) before her towards the door. "First you lead a girl on, and then you want to lead her further still. I suppose it amuses you to see her tears. There's the door, now. Off you go! We want your room, not your company. And what good can you see in him?" she went on, turning to Masha. "Has not your uncle been walking into you to-day already? No; she must stick to her promise, forsooth! 'I will have no one but Basil,' Fool that you are!"

"Yes, I *will* have no one but him! I'll never love any one else! I could kill myself for him!" poor Masha burst out, the tears suddenly gushing forth.

For a while I stood watching her as she wiped away those tears. Then I fell to contemplating Basil attentively, in the hope of finding out what there was in him that she found so attractive; yet, though I sympathised with her sincerely in her grief, I could not for the life of me understand how such a charming creature as I considered her to be could love a man like him.

"When *I* become a man," I thought to myself as I returned to my room, "Petrovskoe shall be mine, and Basil and Masha my servants. Some day, when I am sitting in my study and smoking a pipe, Masha will chance to pass the door on her way to the kitchen with an iron, and I shall say, 'Masha, come here,' and she will enter, and there will be no one else in the room. Then suddenly Basil too will enter, and, on seeing her, will cry, 'My sweetheart is lost to me!' and Masha will begin to weep, Then *I* shall say, 'Basil, I know that you love her, and that she loves you. Here are a thousand roubles for you. Marry her, and may God grant you both happiness!' Then I shall leave them together."

Among the countless thoughts and fancies which pass, without logic or sequence, through the mind and the imagination, there are always some which leave behind them a mark so profound that, without remembering their exact subject, we can at least recall that something good has passed through our brain, and try to retain and reproduce its effect. Such was the mark left upon my consciousness by the idea of sacrificing my feelings to Masha's happiness, seeing that she believed that she could attain it only through a union with Basil.

XIX.
Boyhood

Perhaps people will scarcely believe me when I tell them what were the dearest, most constant, objects of my reflections during my boyhood, so little did those objects consort with my age and position. Yet, in my opinion, contrast between a man's actual position and his moral activity constitutes the most reliable sign of his genuineness.

During the period when I was leading a solitary and self-centred moral life, I was much taken up with abstract thoughts on man's destiny, on a future life, and on the immortality of the soul, and, with all the ardour of inexperience, strove to make my youthful intellect solve those questions—the questions which constitute the highest level of thought to which the human intellect can tend, but a final decision of which the human intellect can never succeed in attaining.

I believe the intellect to take the same course of development in the individual as in the mass, as also that the thoughts which serve as a basis for philosophical theories are an inseparable part of that intellect, and that every man must be more or less conscious of those thoughts before he can know anything of the existence of philosophical theories. To my own mind those thoughts presented themselves with such clarity and force that I tried to apply them to life, in the fond belief that I was the first to have discovered such splendid and invaluable truths.

Sometimes I would suppose that happiness depends, not upon external causes themselves, but only upon our relation to them, and that, provided a man can accustom himself to bearing suffering, he need never be unhappy. To prove the latter hypothesis, I would (despite the horrible pain) hold out a Tatistchev's dictionary at arm's length for five minutes at a time, or else go into the store-room and scourge my back with cords until the tears involuntarily came to my eyes!

Another time, suddenly bethinking me that death might find me at any hour or any minute, I came to the conclusion that man could only be happy by using the present to the full and taking no thought for the future. Indeed, I wondered how people had never found that out before. Acting under the influence of the new idea, I laid my lesson-books aside for two or three days, and, reposing on my bed, gave myself up to novel-reading and the eating of gingerbread-and-honey which I had bought with my last remaining coins.

Again, standing one day before the blackboard and smearing figures on it with honey, I was struck with the thought, "Why is symmetry so agreeable to the eye? What is symmetry? Of course it is an innate sense," I continued; "yet what is its basis? Perhaps everything in life is symmetry? But no. On the contrary, *this* is life"—and I drew an oblong figure on the board—"and after life the soul passes to eternity"—here I drew a line from one end of the oblong figure to the edge of the board. "Why should there not be a corresponding line on the other side? If there be an eternity on one side, there must surely be a corresponding one on the other? That means that we have existed in a previous life, but have lost the recollection of it."

This conclusion—which seemed to me at the time both clear and novel, but the arguments for which it would be difficult for me, at this distance of time, to piece together—pleased me extremely, so I took a piece of paper and tried to write it down. But at the first attempt such a rush of other thoughts came whirling though my brain that I was obliged to jump up and pace the room. At the window, my attention was arrested by a driver harnessing a horse to a water-cart, and at once my mind concentrated itself upon the decision of the question, "Into what animal or human being will the spirit of that horse pass at death?" Just at that moment, Woloda passed through the room, and smiled to see me absorbed in speculative thoughts. His smile at once made me feel that all that I had been thinking about was utter nonsense.

I have related all this as I recollect it in order to show the reader the nature of my cogitations. No philosophical theory attracted me so much as scepticism, which at one period brought me to a state of mind verging upon insanity. I took the fancy into my head that no one nor anything really existed in the world except myself—that objects were not objects at all, but that images of them became manifest only so soon as I turned my attention upon them, and vanished again directly that I ceased to think about them. In short, this idea of mine (that real objects do not exist, but only one's conception of them) brought me to Schelling's well-known theory. There were moments when the influence of this idea led me to such vagaries as, for instance, turning sharply round, in the hope that by the suddenness of the movement I should come in contact with the void which I believed to be existing where I myself purported to be!

What a pitiful spring of moral activity is the human intellect! My faulty reason could not define the impenetrable. Consequently it shattered one fruitless conviction after another—convictions which, happily for my after life, I never lacked the courage to abandon as soon as they proved inadequate. From all this weary mental struggle I derived only a certain pliancy of mind, a weakening of the will, a habit of perpetual moral analysis, and a diminution both of freshness of sentiment and of clearness of thought. Usually abstract thinking develops man's capacity for apprehending the bent of his mind at certain moments and laying it to heart, but my inclination for abstract thought developed my consciousness in such a way that often when I began to consider even the simplest matter, I would lose myself in a labyrinthine analysis of my own thoughts concerning the matter in question. That is to say, I no longer thought of the matter itself, but only of what I was thinking about it. If I had then asked myself, "Of what am I thinking?" the true answer would have been, "I am thinking of what I am thinking;" and if I had further asked myself, "What, then, are the thoughts of which I am thinking?" I should have had to reply, "They are attempts to think of what I am thinking concerning my own thoughts"—and so on. Reason, with me, had to yield to excess of reason. Every philosophical discovery which I made so flattered my conceit that I often imagined myself to be a great man discovering new truths for the benefit of humanity. Consequently, I looked down with proud dignity upon my fellow-mortals. Yet, strange to state, no sooner did I come in contact with those fellow-mortals than I became filled with a stupid shyness of them, and, the higher I happened to be standing in my own opinion, the less did I feel capable of making others perceive my consciousness of my own dignity, since I could not rid myself of a sense of diffidence concerning even the simplest of my words and acts.

XX.
Woloda

The further I advance in the recital of this period of my life, the more difficult and onerous does the task become. Too rarely do I find among the reminiscences of that time any moments full of the ardent feeling of sincerity which so often and so cheeringly illumined my childhood. Gladly would I pass in haste over my lonely boyhood, the sooner to arrive at the happy time when once again a tender, sincere, and noble friendship marked with a gleam of light at once the termination of that period and the beginning of a phase of my youth which was full of the charm of poetry. Therefore, I will not pursue my recollections from hour to hour, but only throw a cursory glance at the most prominent of them, from the time to which I have now carried my tale to the moment of my first contact with the exceptional personality that was fated to exercise such a decisive influence upon my character and ideas.

Woloda was about to enter the University. Tutors came to give him lessons independently of myself, and I listened with envy and involuntary respect as he drew boldly on the blackboard with white chalk and talked about "functions," "sines," and so forth—all of which seemed to me terms pertaining to unattainable wisdom. At length, one Sunday before luncheon all the tutors—and among them two professors—assembled in Grandmamma's room, and in the presence of Papa and some friends put Woloda through a rehearsal of his University examination—in which, to Grandmamma's delight, he gave evidence of no ordinary amount of knowledge.

Questions on different subjects were also put to me, but on all of them I showed complete ignorance, while the fact that the professors manifestly endeavoured to conceal that ignorance from Grandmamma only confused me the more. Yet, after all, I was only fifteen, and so had a year before me in which to prepare for the examinations. Woloda now came downstairs for luncheon only, and spent whole days and evenings over his studies in his own room—to which he kept, not from necessity, but because he preferred its seclusion. He was very ambitious, and meant to pass the examinations, not by halves, but with flying colours.

The first day arrived. Woloda was wearing a new blue frockcoat with brass buttons, a gold watch, and shiny boots. At the door stood Papa's phaeton, which Nicola duly opened; and presently, when Woloda and St. Jerome set out for the University, the girls—particularly Katenka—could be seen gazing with beaming faces from the window at Woloda's pleasing figure as it sat in the carriage. Papa said several times, "God go with him!" and Grandmamma, who also had dragged herself to the window, continued to make the sign of the cross as long as the phaeton was visible, as well as to murmur something to herself.

When Woloda returned, every one eagerly crowded round him. "How many marks? Were they good ones?" "Yes." But his happy face was an answer in itself. He had received five marks—the maximum! The next day, he sped on his way with the same good wishes and the same anxiety for his success, and was welcomed home with the same eagerness and joy.

This lasted for nine days. On the tenth day there was to be the last and most difficult examination of all—the one in divinity.

We all stood at the window, and watched for him with greater impatience than ever. Two o'clock, and yet no Woloda.

"Here they come, Papa! Here they come!" suddenly screamed Lubotshka as she peered through the window.

Sure enough the phaeton was driving up with St. Jerome and Woloda—the latter no longer in his grey cap and blue frockcoat, but in the uniform of a student of the University, with its embroidered blue collar, three-cornered hat, and gilded sword.

"Ah! If only *she* had been alive now!" exclaimed Grandmamma on seeing Woloda in this dress, and swooned away.

Woloda enters the anteroom with a beaming face, and embraces myself, Lubotshka, Mimi, and Katenka—the latter blushing to her ears. He hardly knows himself for joy. And how smart he looks in that uniform! How well the blue collar suits his budding, dark moustache! What a tall, elegant figure is his, and what a distinguished walk!

On that memorable day we all lunched together in Grandmamma's room. Every face expressed delight, and with the dessert which followed the meal the servants, with grave but gratified faces, brought in bottles of champagne.

Grandmamma, for the first time since Mamma's death, drank a full glass of the wine to Woloda's health, and wept for joy as she looked at him.

Henceforth Woloda drove his own turn-out, invited his own friends, smoked, and went to balls. On one occasion, I even saw him sharing a couple of bottles of champagne with some guests in his room, and the whole company drinking a toast, with each glass, to some mysterious being, and then quarrelling as to who should have the bottom of the bottle!

Nevertheless he always lunched at home, and after the meal would stretch himself on a sofa and talk confidentially to Katenka: yet from what I overheard (while pretending, of course, to pay no attention) I gathered that they were only talking of the heroes and heroines of novels which they had read, or else of jealousy and love, and so on. Never could I understand what they found so attractive in these conversations, nor why they smiled so happily and discussed things with such animation.

Altogether I could see that, in addition to the friendship natural to persons who had been companions from childhood, there existed between Woloda and Katenka a relation which differentiated them from us, and united them mysteriously to one another.

XXI.
Katenka And Lubotshka

Katenka was now sixteen years old—quite a grown-up girl; and although at that age the angular figures, the bashfulness, and the *gaucherie* peculiar to girls passing from childhood to youth usually replace the comely freshness and graceful, half-developed bloom of childhood, she had in no way altered. Still the blue eyes with their merry glance were hers, the well-shaped nose with firm nostrils and almost forming a line with the forehead, the little mouth with its charming smile, the dimples in the rosy cheeks, and the small white hands. To her, the epithet of "girl," pure and simple, was pre-eminently applicable, for in her the only new features were a new and "young-lady-like" arrangement of her thick flaxen hair and a youthful bosom—the latter an addition which at once caused her great joy and made her very bashful.

Although Lubotshka and she had grown up together and received the same education, they were totally unlike one another. Lubotshka was not tall, and the rickets from which she had suffered had shaped her feet in goose fashion and made her figure very bad. The only pretty feature in her face was her eyes, which were indeed wonderful, being large and black, and instinct with such an extremely pleasing expression of mingled gravity and *naïveté* that she was bound to attract attention. In everything she was simple and natural, so that, whereas Katenka always looked as though she were trying to be like some one else, Lubotshka looked people straight in the face, and sometimes fixed them so long with her splendid black eyes that she got blamed for doing what was thought to be improper. Katenka, on the contrary, always cast her eyelids down, blinked, and pretended that she was short-sighted, though I knew very well that her sight was excellent. Lubotshka hated being shown off before strangers, and when a visitor offered to kiss her she invariably grew cross, and said that she hated "affection"; whereas, when strangers were present, Katenka was always particularly endearing to Mimi, and loved to walk about the room arm in arm with another girl. Likewise, though Lubotshka was a terrible giggler, and sometimes ran about the room in convulsions of gesticulating laughter, Katenka always covered her mouth with her hands or her pocket-handkerchief when she wanted to laugh. Lubotshka, again, loved to have grown-up men to talk to, and said that some day she meant to marry a hussar, but Katenka always pretended that all men were horrid, and that she never meant to marry any one of them, while as soon as a male visitor addressed her she changed completely, as though she were nervous of something. Likewise, Lubotshka was continually at loggerheads with Mimi because the latter wanted her to have her stays so tight that she could not breathe or eat or drink in comfort, while Katenka, on the contrary, would often insert her finger into her waistband to show how loose it was, and always ate very little. Lubotshka liked to draw heads; Katenka only flowers and butterflies. The former could play Field's concertos and Beethoven's sonatas excellently, whereas the latter indulged in variations and waltzes, retarded the time, and used the pedals continuously—not to mention the fact that, before she began, she invariably struck three chords in *arpeggio*.

Nevertheless, in those days I thought Katenka much the grander person of the two, and liked her the best.

XXII.
Papa

Papa had been in a particularly good humour ever since Woloda had passed into the University, and came much oftener to dine with Grandmamma. However, I knew from Nicola that he had won a great deal lately. Occasionally, he would come and sit with us in the evening before going to the club. He used to sit down to the piano and bid us group ourselves around him, after which he would beat time with his thin boots (he detested heels, and never wore them), and make us sing gipsy songs. At such times you should have seen the quaint enthusiasm of his beloved Lubotshka, who adored him!

Sometimes, again, he would come to the schoolroom and listen with a grave face as I said my lessons; yet by the few words which he would let drop when correcting me, I could see that he knew even less about the subject than I did. Not infrequently, too, he would wink at us and make secret signs when Grandmamma was beginning to scold us and find fault with us all round. "So much for us children!" he would say. On the whole, however, the impossible pinnacle upon which my childish imagination had placed him had undergone a certain abasement. I still kissed his large white hand with a certain feeling of love and respect, but I also allowed myself to think about him and to criticise his behaviour until involuntarily thoughts occurred to me which alarmed me by their presence. Never shall I forget one incident in particular which awakened thoughts of this kind, and caused me intense astonishment. Late one evening, he entered the drawing-room in his black dress-coat and white waistcoat, to take Woloda (who was still dressing in his bedroom) to a ball. Grandmamma was also in her bedroom, but had given orders that, before setting out, Woloda was to come and say goodbye to her (it was her invariable custom to inspect him before he went to a ball, and to bless him and direct him as to his behaviour). The room where we were was lighted by a solitary lamp. Mimi and Katenka were walking up and down, and Lubotshka was playing Field's Second Concerto (Mamma's favourite piece) at the piano. Never was there such a family likeness as between Mamma and my sister—not so much in the face or the stature as in the hands, the walk, the voice, the favourite expressions, and, above all, the way of playing the piano and the whole demeanour at the instrument. Lubotshka always arranged her dress when sitting down just as Mamma had done, as well as turned the leaves like her, tapped her fingers angrily and said "Dear me!" whenever a difficult passage did not go smoothly, and, in particular, played with the delicacy and exquisite purity of touch which in those days caused the execution of Field's music to be known characteristically as "*jeu perlé*" and to lie beyond comparison with the humbug of our modern *virtuosi*.

Papa entered the room with short, soft steps, and approached Lubotshka. On seeing him she stopped playing.

"No, go on, Luba, go on," he said as he forced her to sit down again. She went on playing, while Papa, his head on his hand, sat near her for a while. Then suddenly he gave his shoulders a shrug, and, rising, began to pace the room. Every time that he approached the piano he halted for a moment and looked fixedly at Lubotshka. By his walk and his every movement, I could see that he was greatly agitated. Once, when he stopped behind Lubotshka, he kissed her black hair, and then, wheeling quickly round, resumed his pacing. The piece finished, Lubotshka went up to him and said, "Was it well played?" whereupon, without answering, he took her head in his two hands, and kissed her forehead and eyes with such tenderness as I had never before seen him display.

"Why, you are crying!" cried Lubotshka suddenly as she ceased to toy with his watch-chain and stared at him with her great black eyes. "Pardon me, darling Papa! I had quite forgotten that it was dear Mamma's piece which I was playing."

"No, no, my love; play it often," he said in a voice trembling with emotion. "Ah, if you only knew how much good it does me to share your tears!"

He kissed her again, and then, mastering his feelings and shrugging his shoulders, went to the door leading to the corridor which ran past Woloda's room.

"Waldemar, shall you be ready soon?" he cried, halting in the middle of the passage. Just then Masha came along.

"Why, you look prettier every day," he said to her. She blushed and passed on.

"Waldemar, shall you be ready soon?" he cried again, with a cough and a shake of his shoulders, just as Masha slipped away and he first caught sight of me.

I loved Papa, but the intellect is independent of the heart, and often gives birth to thoughts which offend and are harsh and incomprehensible to the feelings. And it was thoughts of this kind that, for all I strove to put them away, arose at that moment in my mind.

XXIII. Grandmamma

Grandmamma was growing weaker every day. Her bell, Gasha's grumbling voice, and the slamming of doors in her room were sounds of constant occurrence, and she no longer received us sitting in the Voltairian arm-chair in her boudoir, but lying on the bed in her bedroom, supported on lace-trimmed cushions. One day when she greeted us, I noticed a yellowish-white swelling on her hand, and smelt the same oppressive odour which I had smelt five years ago in Mamma's room. The doctor came three times a day, and there had been more than one consultation. Yet the character of her haughty, ceremonious bearing towards all who lived with her, and particularly towards Papa, never changed in the least. She went on emphasising certain words, raising her eyebrows, and saying "my dear," just as she had always done.

Then for a few days we did not see her at all, and one morning St. Jerome proposed to me that Woloda and I should take Katenka and Lubotshka for a drive during the hours generally allotted to study. Although I observed that the street was lined with straw under the windows of Grandmamma's room, and that some men in blue stockings[1] were standing at our gate, the reason never dawned upon me why we were being sent out at that unusual hour. Throughout the drive Lubotshka and I were in that particularly merry mood when the least trifle, the least word or movement, sets one off laughing.

A pedlar went trotting across the road with a tray, and we laughed. Some ragged cabmen, brandishing their reins and driving at full speed, overtook our sledge, and we laughed again. Next, Philip's whip got caught in the side of the vehicle, and the way in which he said, "Bother the thing!" as he drove to disentangle it almost killed us with mirth. Mimi looked displeased, and said that only silly people laughed for no reason at all, but Lubotshka—her face purple with suppressed merriment—

[1] Undertaker's men.

needed but to give me a sly glance, and we again burst out into such Homeric laughter, when our eyes met, that the tears rushed into them and we could not stop our paroxysms, although they nearly choked us. Hardly, again, had we desisted a little when I looked at Lubotshka once more, and gave vent to one of the slang words which we then affected among ourselves—words which always called forth hilarity; and in a moment we were laughing again.

Just as we reached home, I was opening my mouth to make a splendid grimace at Lubotshka when my eye fell upon a black coffin-cover which was leaning against the gate—and my mouth remained fixed in its gaping position.

"Your Grandmamma is dead," said St. Jerome as he met us. His face was very pale.

Throughout the whole time that Grandmamma's body was in the house I was oppressed with the fear of death, for the corpse served as a forcible and disagreeable reminder that I too must die some day—a feeling which people often mistake for grief. I had no sincere regret for Grandmamma, nor, I think, had any one else, since, although the house was full of sympathising callers, nobody seemed to mourn for her from their hearts except one mourner whose genuine grief made a great impression upon me, seeing that the mourner in question was—Gasha! She shut herself up in the garret, tore her hair and refused all consolation, saying that, now that her mistress was dead, she only wished to die herself.

I again assert that, in matters of feeling, it is the unexpected effects that constitute the most reliable signs of sincerity.

Though Grandmamma was no longer with us, reminiscences and gossip about her long went on in the house. Such gossip referred mostly to her will, which she had made shortly before her death, and of which, as yet, no one knew the contents except her bosom friend, Prince Ivan Ivanovitch. I could hear the servants talking excitedly together, and making innumerable conjectures as to the amount left and the probable beneficiaries: nor can I deny that the idea that we ourselves were probably the latter greatly pleased me.

Six weeks later, Nicola—who acted as regular news-agent to the house—informed me that Grandmamma had left the whole of her fortune to Lubotshka, with, as her trustee until her majority, not Papa, but Prince Ivan Ivanovitch!

XXIV.
Myself

Only a few months remained before I was to matriculate for the University, yet I was making such good progress that I felt no apprehensions, and even took a pleasure in my studies. I kept in good heart, and learnt my lessons fluently and intelligently. The faculty I had selected was the mathematical one—probably, to tell the truth, because the terms "tangent," "differentials," "integrals," and so forth, pleased my fancy.

Though stout and broad-shouldered, I was shorter than Woloda, while my ugliness of face still remained and tormented me as much as ever. By way of compensation, I tried to appear original. Yet one thing comforted me, namely, that Papa had said that I had "an *intelligent* face." I quite believed him.

St. Jerome was not only satisfied with me, but actually had taken to praising me. Consequently, I had now ceased to hate him. In fact, when, one day, he said that, with my "capacities" and my "intellect," it would be shameful for me not to accomplish this, that, or the other thing, I believe I almost liked him.

I had long ago given up keeping observation on the maidservants' room, for I was now ashamed to hide behind doors. Likewise, I confess that the knowledge of Masha's love for Basil had greatly cooled my ardour for her, and that my passion underwent a final cure by their marriage—a consummation to which I myself contributed by, at Basil's request, asking Papa's consent to the union.

When the newly-married couple brought trays of cakes and sweetmeats to Papa as a thank-offering, and Masha, in a cap with blue ribbons, kissed each of us on the shoulder in token of her gratitude, I merely noticed the scent of the rose pomade on her hair, but felt no other sensation.

In general, I was beginning to get the better of my youthful defects, with the exception of the principal one—the one of which I shall often again have to speak in relating my life's history—namely, the tendency to abstract thought.

XXV.
Woloda's Friends

Although, when in the society of Woloda's friends, I had to play a part that hurt my pride, I liked sitting in his room when he had visitors, and silently watching all they did. The two who came most frequently to see him were a military adjutant called Dubkoff and a student named Prince Nechludoff. Dubkoff was a little dark-haired, highly-strung man who, though short of stature and no longer in his first youth, had a pleasing and invariably cheerful air. His was one of those limited natures which are agreeable through their very limitations; natures which cannot regard matters from every point of view, but which are nevertheless attracted by everything. Usually the reasoning of such persons is false and one-sided, yet always genuine and taking; wherefore their narrow egotism seems both amiable and excusable. There were two other reasons why Dubkoff had charms for Woloda and myself—namely, the fact that he was of military appearance, and, secondly (and principally), the fact that he was of a certain age—an age with which young people are apt to associate that quality of "gentlemanliness" which is so highly esteemed at their time of life. However, he was in very truth *un homme comme il faut*. The only thing which I did not like about it all was that, in his presence, Woloda always seemed ashamed of my innocent behaviour, and still more so of my youthfulness. As for Prince Nechludoff, he was in no way handsome, since neither his small grey eyes, his low, projecting forehead, nor his disproportionately long hands and feet could be called good features. The only good points about him were his unusually tall stature, his delicate colouring, and his splendid teeth. Nevertheless, his face was of such an original, energetic character (owing to his narrow, sparkling eyes and ever-changing expression—now stern, now childlike, now smiling indeterminately) that it was impossible to help noticing it. As a rule he was very shy, and would blush to the ears at the smallest trifle, but it was a shyness altogether different from mine, seeing that, the more he blushed, the more determined-looking he grew, as though he were vexed at his own weakness.

Although he was on very good terms with Woloda and Dubkoff, it was clearly chance which had united them thus, since their tastes were entirely dissimilar. Woloda and Dubkoff seemed to be afraid of anything like serious consideration or emotion, whereas Nechludoff was beyond all things an enthusiast, and would often, despite their sarcastic remarks, plunge into dissertations on philosophical matters or matters of feeling. Again, the two former liked talking about the fair objects of their adoration (these were always numerous, and always shared by the friends in common), whereas Nechludoff invariably grew annoyed when taxed with his love for a certain red-haired lady.

Again, Woloda and Dubkoff often permitted themselves to criticise their relatives, and to find amusement in so doing, but Nechludoff flew into a tremendous rage when on one occasion they referred to some weak points in the character of an aunt of his whom he adored. Finally, after supper Woloda and Dubkoff would usually go off to some place whither Nechludoff would not accompany them; wherefore they called him "a dainty girl."

The very first time that I ever saw Prince Nechludoff I was struck with his exterior and conversation. Yet, though I could discern a great similarity between his disposition and my own (or perhaps it was because I *could* so discern it), the impression which he produced upon me at first was anything but agreeable. I liked neither his quick glance, his hard voice, his proud bearing, nor (least of all) the utter indifference with which he treated me. Often, when conversing, I burned to contradict him, to punish his pride by confuting him, to show him that I was clever in spite of his disdainful neglect of my presence. But I was invariably prevented from doing so by my shyness.

XXVI.
Discussions

Woloda was lying reading a French novel on the sofa when I paid my usual visit to his room after my evening lessons. He looked up at me for a moment from his book, and then went on reading. This perfectly simple and natural movement, however, offended me. I conceived that the glance implied a question why I had come and a wish to hide his thoughts from me (I may say that at that period a tendency to attach a meaning to the most insignificant of acts formed a prominent feature in my character). So I went to the table and also took up a book to read. Yet, even before I had actually begun reading, the idea struck me how ridiculous it was that, although we had never seen one another all day, we should have not a word to exchange.

"Are you going to stay in to-night, Woloda?"

"I don't know. Why?"

"Oh, because—" Seeing that the conversation did not promise to be a success, I took up my book again, and began to read. Yet it was a strange thing that, though we sometimes passed whole hours together without speaking when we were alone, the mere presence of a third—sometimes of a taciturn and wholly uninteresting person—sufficed to plunge us into the most varied and engrossing of discussions. The truth was that we knew one another too well, and to know a person either too well or too little acts as a bar to intimacy.

"Is Woloda at home?" came in Dubkoff's voice from the ante-room.

"Yes!" shouted Woloda, springing up and throwing aside his book.

Dubkoff and Nechludoff entered.

"Are you coming to the theatre, Woloda?"

"No, I have no time," he replied with a blush.

"Oh, never mind that. Come along."

"But I haven't got a ticket."

"Tickets, as many as you like, at the entrance."

"Very well, then; I'll be back in a minute," said Woloda evasively as he left the room. I knew very well that he wanted to go, but that he had declined because he had no money, and had now gone to borrow five roubles of one of the servants—to be repaid when he got his next allowance.

"How do you do, *diplomat?*" said Dubkoff to me as he shook me by the hand. Woloda's friends had called me by that nickname since the day when Grandmamma had said at luncheon that Woloda must go into the army, but that she would like to see me in the diplomatic service, dressed in a black frock-coat, and with my hair arranged *à la coq* (the two essential requirements, in her opinion, of a *diplomat*).

"Where has Woloda gone to?" asked Nechludoff.

"I don't know," I replied, blushing to think that nevertheless they had probably guessed his errand.

"I suppose he has no money? Yes, I can see I am right, O diplomatist," he added, taking my smile as an answer in the affirmative. "Well, I have none, either. Have you any, Dubkoff?"

"I'll see," replied Dubkoff, feeling for his pocket, and rummaging gingerly about with his squat little fingers among his small change. "Yes, here are five copecks-twenty, but that's all," he concluded with a comic gesture of his hand.

At this point Woloda re-entered.

"Are we going?"

"No."

"What an odd fellow you are!" said Nechludoff. "Why don't you say that you have no money? Here, take my ticket."

"But what are *you* going to do?"

"He can go into his cousin's box," said Dubkoff.

"No, I'm not going at all," replied Nechludoff.

"Why?"

"Because I hate sitting in a box."

"And for what reason?"

"I don't know. Somehow I feel uncomfortable there."

"Always the same! I can't understand a fellow feeling uncomfortable when he is sitting with people who are fond of him. It is unnatural, *mon cher.*"

"But what else is there to be done *si je suis tant timide? You* never blushed in your life, but I do at the least trifle," and he blushed at that moment.

"Do you know what that nervousness of yours proceeds from?" said Dubkoff in a protecting sort of tone, "*D'un excés d'amour propre, mon cher.*"

"What do you mean by '*excés d'amour propre*'?" asked Nechludoff, highly offended. "On the contrary, I am shy just because I have *too little amour propre*. I always feel as though I were being tiresome and disagreeable, and therefore—"

"Well, get ready, Woloda," interrupted Dubkoff, tapping my brother on the shoulder and handing him his cloak. "Ignaz, get your master ready."

"Therefore," continued Nechludoff, "it often happens with me that—"

But Dubkoff was not listening. "Tra-la-la-la," and he hummed a popular air.

"Oh, but I'm not going to let you off," went on Nechludoff. "I mean to prove to you that my shyness is not the result of conceit."

"You can prove it as we go along."

"But I have told you that I am *not* going."

"Well, then, stay here and prove it to the *diplomat*, and he can tell us all about it when we return."

"Yes, that's what I *will* do," said Nechludoff with boyish obstinacy, "so hurry up with your return."

"Well, *do* you think I am egotistic?" he continued, seating himself beside me.

True, I had a definite opinion on the subject, but I felt so taken aback by this unexpected question that at first I could make no reply.

"Yes, I *do* think so," I said at length in a faltering voice, and colouring at the thought that at last the moment had come when I could show him that I was clever. "I think that *everybody* is egotistic, and that everything we do is done out of egotism."

"But what do you call egotism?" asked Nechludoff—smiling, as I thought, a little contemptuously.

"Egotism is a conviction that we are better and cleverer than any one else," I replied.

"But how can we *all* be filled with this conviction?" he inquired.

"Well, I don't know if I am right or not—certainly no one but myself seems to hold the opinion—but I believe that I am wiser than any one else in the world, and that all of you know it."

"At least I can say for myself," observed Nechludoff, "that I have met a *few* people whom I believe to excel me in wisdom."

"It is impossible," I replied with conviction.

"Do you really think so?" he said, looking at me gravely.

"Yes, really," I answered, and an idea crossed my mind which I proceeded to expound further. "Let me prove it to you. Why do we love ourselves better than any one else? Because we think ourselves *better* than any one else—more worthy of our own love. If we *thought* others better than ourselves, we should *love* them better than ourselves: but that is never the case. And even if it were so, I should still be right," I added with an involuntary smile of complacency.

For a few minutes Nechludoff was silent.

"I never thought you were so clever," he said with a smile so goodhumoured and charming that I at once felt happy.

Praise exercises an all potent influence, not only upon the feelings, but also upon the intellect; so that under the influence of that agreeable sensation I straightway felt much cleverer than before, and thoughts began to rush with extraordinary rapidity through my head. From egotism we passed insensibly to the theme of love, which seemed inexhaustible. Although our reasonings might have sounded nonsensical to a listener (so vague and one-sided were they), for ourselves they had a profound significance. Our minds were so perfectly in harmony that not a chord was struck in the one without awakening an echo in the other, and in this harmonious striking of different chords we found the greatest delight. Indeed, we felt as though time and language were insufficient to express the thoughts which seethed within us.

XXVII.
The Beginning of Our Friendship

From that time forth, a strange, but exceedingly pleasant, relation subsisted between Dimitri Nechludoff and myself. Before other people he paid me scanty attention, but as soon as ever we were alone, we would sit down together in some comfortable corner and, forgetful both of time and of everything around us, fall to reasoning.

We talked of a future life, of art, service, marriage, and education; nor did the idea ever occur to us that very possibly all we said was shocking nonsense. The reason why it never occurred to us was that the nonsense which we talked was good, sensible nonsense, and that, so long as one is young, one can appreciate good nonsense, and believe in it. In youth the powers of the mind are directed wholly to the future, and that future assumes such various, vivid, and alluring forms under the influence of hope—hope based, not upon the experience of the past, but upon an assumed possibility of happiness to come—that such dreams of expected felicity constitute in themselves the true happiness of that period of our life. How I loved those moments in our metaphysical discussions (discussions which formed the major portion of our intercourse) when thoughts came thronging faster and faster, and, succeeding one another at lightning speed, and growing more and more abstract, at length attained such a pitch of elevation that one felt powerless to express them, and said something quite different from what one had intended at first to say! How I liked those moments, too, when, carried higher and higher into the realms of thought, we suddenly felt that we could grasp its substance no longer and go no further!

At carnival time Nechludoff was so much taken up with one festivity and another that, though he came to see us several times a day, he never addressed a single word to me. This offended me so much that once again I found myself thinking him a haughty, disagreeable fellow, and only awaited an opportunity to show him that I no longer valued his company or felt any particular affection for him. Accordingly, the first time that he spoke to me after the carnival, I said that I had lessons to do, and went upstairs, but a quarter of an hour later some one opened the schoolroom door, and Nechludoff entered.

"Am I disturbing you?" he asked.

"No," I replied, although I had at first intended to say that I had a great deal to do.

"Then why did you run away just now? It is a long while since we had a talk together, and I have grown so accustomed to these discussions that I feel as though something were wanting."

My anger had quite gone now, and Dimitri stood before me the same good and lovable being as before.

"You know, perhaps, why I ran away?" I said.

"Perhaps I do," he answered, taking a seat near me. "However, though it is possible I know why, I cannot say it straight out, whereas *you* can."

"Then I will do so. I ran away because I was angry with you—well, not angry, but grieved. I always have an idea that you despise me for being so young."

"Well, do you know why *I* always feel so attracted towards you?" he replied, meeting my confession with a look of kind understanding, "and why I like you better than any of my other acquaintances or than any of the people among whom I mostly have to live? It is because I found out at once that you have the rare and astonishing gift of sincerity."

"Yes, I always confess the things of which I am most ashamed—but only to people in whom I trust," I said.

"Ah, but to trust a man you must be his friend *completely*, and we are not friends yet, Nicolas. Remember how, when we were speaking of friendship, we agreed that, to be real friends, we ought to trust one another implicitly."

"I trust you in so far as that I feel convinced that you would never repeat a word of what I might tell you," I said.

"Yet perhaps the most interesting and important thoughts of all are just those which we never tell one another, while the mean thoughts (the thoughts which, if we only knew that we had to confess them to one another, would probably never have the hardihood to enter our minds)—Well, do you know what I am thinking of, Nicolas?" he broke off, rising and taking my hand with a smile. "I propose (and I feel sure that it would benefit us mutually) that we should pledge our word to one another to tell each other *everything*. We should then really know each other, and never have anything on our consciences. And, to guard against outsiders, let us also agree never to speak of one another to a third person. Suppose we do that?"

"I agree," I replied. And we did it. What the result was shall be told hereafter.

Kerr has said that every attachment has two sides: one loves, and the other allows himself to be loved; one kisses, and the other surrenders his cheek. That is perfectly true. In the case of our own attachment it was I who kissed, and Dimitri who surrendered his cheek—though he, in his turn, was ready to pay me a similar salute. We loved equally because we knew and appreciated each other thoroughly, but this did not prevent him from exercising an influence over me, nor myself from rendering him adoration.

It will readily be understood that Nechludoff's influence caused me to adopt his bent of mind, the essence of which lay in an enthusiastic reverence for ideal virtue and a firm belief in man's vocation to perpetual perfection. To raise mankind, to abolish vice and misery, seemed at that time a task offering no difficulties. To educate oneself to every virtue, and so to achieve happiness, seemed a simple and easy matter.

Only God Himself knows whether those blessed dreams of youth were ridiculous, or whose the fault was that they never became realised.

THE END

www.ingramcontent.com/pod-product-compliance
Ingram Content Group UK Ltd.
Pitfield, Milton Keynes, MK11 3LW, UK
UKHW040318300826
14791UKWH00003B/964

9 789354 629518